W9-CHH-716

"I cannot imagine that there are many pastors who have not heard each of the six questions that Graham Cole raises. Here are serious, careful, practical, theologically-alert answers. This book deserves the widest circulation."

—D. A. CARSON, Research Professor of New Testament, Trinity Evangelical Divinity School

"Pneumatology has been sadly neglected in recent evangelical theology and, when it has been touched upon, it has trended toward either the speculative or the sensational. But here is a book on the Holy Spirit that is practical, relevant, balanced, and useful in the lives of God's people everywhere. This book provides important grounding for a fuller theology of the Holy Spirit, and I commend it to all believers who are serious about the Christian life."

—TIMOTHY GEORGE, Dean, Beeson Divinity School, Samford University; Senior Editor, *Christianity Today*

"Drawing from the well of his extensive and rigorous study of the doctrine of the Holy Spirit, Dr. Graham Cole gives refreshingly clear answers to six crucial questions that earnest Christians invariably ask about the Holy Spirit. The answers are sure to grace the church, because what Christians believe about the third Person of the Holy Trinity will determine how they live. This is an important, accessible, life-giving book."

—R. KENT HUGHES, Senior Pastor Emeritus, College Church, Wheaton, Illinois

"Dr. Graham Cole's book makes a significant contribution to the life of the church. Uncertainty about the person of the Holy Spirit sometimes leads to division in the local church and often to confusion in the life of the individual believer. I have found in my pastoral calling that the challenges churches face about the doctrine of the Spirit all come back to the six questions Dr. Cole addresses. In fact, his subtitle is an accurate description of this insight-filled book—*real questions, practical answers*. Dr. Cole handles all the relevant biblical texts carefully and accurately and then places his findings into a coherent theological framework. He distills the views about the Holy Spirit that have been held by brothers and sisters in Christ of the past. Then, with clarity and relevance, he points out how his biblical, theological, and historical findings might be applied to the concerns church people face in their daily lives and in their understanding of the triune God. I believe every pastor, Christian counselor, and lay leader should keep this book close at hand. When churches wrestle with division over contradictory views related to the work of the Holy Spirit, this book will provide lucid and succinct guidance. When individuals fear they have sinned against or grieved the Holy Spirit, Dr. Cole's teaching will provide clarity and encouragement. When church leaders long for their congregations to know the filling of the Spirit of God, they will find, in this book, wisdom. I recommend it highly."

—GREG WAYBRIGHT, Former President, Trinity Evangelical Divinity School; Senior Pastor, Lake Avenue Church, Pasadena, California

ENGAGING *with the*
HOLY SPIRIT
REAL QUESTIONS, PRACTICAL ANSWERS

GRAHAM A. COLE
Foreword by David Peterson

CROSSWAY BOOKS
WHEATON, ILLINOIS

Library of Congress Cataloging-in-Publication Data

Cole, Graham A. (Graham Arthur), 1949–
    Engaging with the Holy Spirit : real questions, practical
answers / Graham A. Cole.
        p. cm.
    Includes bibliographical references and index.
    ISBN 978-1-58134-972-6 (tpb)
    1. Holy Spirit. I. Title.
BT121.3.C645   2008
231'.3—dc22   2007044604

VP		17	16	15	14	13	12	11	10	09	08
15	14	13	12	11	10	9	8	7	6	5	4	3	2	1

To those special people:
my beloved Jules, Jonathan and Eva,
Jerome and Judith, Hannah and Isaiah.

CONTENTS

FOREWORD

DESPITE THE MANY BOOKS that have been written on the subject in recent decades, the person and work of the Holy Spirit remains a fascinating area for further exploration. Graham Cole has focused his research firstly on ways in which we may sin against the Spirit, secondly on whether it is right to pray to the Spirit, and thirdly on what it means to be filled with the Spirit. Each chapter confronts us with important challenges about our relationship with the Spirit, either as believers or as unbelievers.

However, in fulfilling his aims, Graham has also enriched us with some valuable reflections on theological method. How do we handle the biblical evidence reverently and responsibly? How do we interpret the Bible's teaching in the light of many centuries of differing insights and opinions? In particular, can we agree on an approach to certain biblical texts about the Spirit? Graham shows us in practice how valuable it is to have a clearly defined and articulated theological method that takes the biblical text seriously, learns from others in the process of interpretation, and works hard at application to the contemporary context.

This is exactly what we hope for at our Annual School of Theology, where college graduates and others come together for a day to reflect on their ministries and to be inspired in their pastoring and teaching of others. We were blessed at Oak Hill by Graham's lectures in 2006 and it is my prayer that many readers will be similarly blessed by the publication of this expanded version of his work.

David Peterson
Principal, Oak Hill Theological College,
London

ACKNOWLEDGMENTS

MY THANKS GO TO the Principal of Oak Hill College, Dr. David G. Peterson, for the gracious invitation to deliver the lectures for the college's annual theology conference. The hospitality was superb. I also owe a great debt of gratitude to Dr. Hans Madueme for his careful proofreading of the text and many helpful comments. Any errors remain my own.

Graham A. Cole

ABBREVIATIONS

CJCC   *The Comprehensive John Calvin Collection* (Rio, WI: Ages Software, 2002), CD-Rom version. The edition of Calvin's *Institutes of the Christian Religion* used is that edited by John T. McNeill and translated by Ford Lewis Battles (Westminster Press, 1960).

DJG   *Dictionary of Jesus and the Gospels*, Joel B. Green and Scot McKnight, eds. (Downers Grove, IL: InterVarsity; Leicester: Inter-Varsity, 1992), *EIRC*.

DLNTD   *The Dictionary of the Later New Testament and its Developments*, Ralph P. Martin and Peter H. Davids, eds. (Downers Grove, IL: InterVarsity; Leicester: Inter-Varsity, 1997), *EIRC*.

EBC   *The Expositor's Bible Commentary*, Frank E. Gaebelein, ed. (Grand Rapids, MI: Zondervan, 1976–), CD-Rom version.

EDT   *Evangelical Dictionary of Theology*, Walter A. Elwell, ed. (Grand Rapids, MI: Baker Books, 1994).

EIRC   *The Essential IVP Reference Collection* (Leicester: Inter-Varsity, 2001), CD-Rom version.

ESV   English Standard Version of the Bible

IBBCNT   *IVP Bible Background Commentary: New Testament*, Craig S. Keener (Downers Grove, IL, InterVarsity, 1993), *EIRC*.

NBCRev   *New Bible Commentary: 21st Century Edition*, D. A. Carson, ed. et al. (Leicester: Inter-Varsity; Downers Grove, IL: InterVarsity, 1994), *EIRC*.

NDBT   *New Dictionary of Biblical Theology*, T. D. Alexander and Brian S. Rosner, eds. (Leicester: Inter-Varsity; Downers Grove, IL: InterVarsity, 2000), *EIRC*.

NDOT   *New Dictionary of Theology*, Sinclair B. Ferguson and David F. Wright, eds. (Leicester: Inter-Varsity; Downers Grove, IL: InterVarsity, 1988), *EIRC*.

NIV   New International Version of the Bible

NRSV   New Revised Standard Version of the Bible

TB   *Tyndale Bulletin*

WBC   *Word Biblical Commentary*, Bruce M. Metzger, David A. Hubbard and Glenn W. Barker, eds. (Nelson Reference & Electronic, 2004), CD-Rom version.

INTRODUCTION

IN THEIR 1967 PUBLICATION, *The Spirit within You: The Church's Neglected Possession*, A. M. Stibbs and J. I. Packer wrote: "'No, we have never even heard that there is a Holy Spirit.' Such was the reply of the Ephesian disciples to St. Paul's question, 'Did you receive the Holy Spirit when you believed?' (Acts 19:2). Their words express a state of mind to which the modern church, to put it mildly, is no stranger."[1] The rise of the charismatic movement and the growth of Pentecostal churches worldwide soon made their comment out of date. In fact, twenty years later when Watson E. Mills compiled a bibliography of assorted works on the Holy Spirit, there were 2,098 entries.[2] One can only imagine how much larger such a bibliography would be by now. The doctrine of the Holy Spirit is no longer neglected.

Even so, real questions remain concerning the Holy Spirit, especially with regards to sinning against the Spirit. What sort of questions? To start with, how may the Holy Spirit be blasphemed? This is a particularly important question, since it troubles numbers of Christians. It is the so-called unpardonable sin. Can Christians commit it, or is it the sin of the outsider? Again, how may the Spirit be resisted? Is this a sin that a person is even conscious of committing? What is its character? These questions arise from reading the biblical text. The next question does not. Rather it stems from the practice of some Christians of praying to the Holy Spirit. Ought we to do so? There are no biblical commands as such to pray to the Spirit. There are no biblical precedents. For example, we do not read of David praying to the Spirit in the Old Testament or Paul praying to the Spirit in the New. What are we to make of the

---

[1] A. M. Stibbs and J. I. Packer, *The Spirit within You: The Church's Neglected Possession* (London: Hodder and Stoughton, 1967), 9. Note the subtitle.
[2] Watson E. Mills, *The Holy Spirit: A Bibliography* (Peabody, MA: Hendrickson, 1988), cited in Craig S. Keener, *3 Crucial Questions about the Holy Spirit* (Grand Rapids, MI: Baker Books, 1996), 203.

practice? The remaining three questions return us to the text of the
New Testament. What does it mean to quench the Spirit? How may
the Holy Spirit be grieved? Finally, what does it mean to be filled by
the Spirit? I have left this question to last as it ends the discussion
on a positive note.

Such questions are the burden of this book, which began life as
the Annual Oak Hill Lectures for 2006. Each question has a chapter
devoted to it and may stand alone. In other words, the reader can
begin anywhere. There is logic, though, to the sequence. The question about blaspheming the Holy Spirit is raised by the Gospels, that
of resisting the Spirit by the book of Acts, and the rest of the questions emanate from the Epistles. Thus we move through the major
kinds of literature found in the New Testament canon. "Gospel"
and "apostle" is how the early church termed it.[3] Only the book of
Revelation as a literary genre is left out.

This brief work is an exercise in doing applied theology. At various points in the unfolding discussion I will draw attention to key
elements in thinking theologically, and some of the implications for
belief and behavior will be explored. The structure of each address
will be the same: after an introduction I will draw attention to some
past and present perspectives on the topic. Some of the great names
of the past and present will figure: Augustine, Calvin, Owen, and
Barth, to give only some examples. Next we engage the biblical testimony on the question before offering a theological reflection on
what we have seen. All this will be followed by a brief conclusion,
as will the work as a whole.

Thinking theologically involves several important components.
Logically speaking, *the word of revelation* is foundational. Scripture
as special revelation from God—albeit in human words—is the
norm of norms. Scripture is the key to Christian quality assurance.
If the ideas in this work are not faithfully and responsibly based
in the Bible or consistent with the scriptural testimony then they
ought to be rejected. However, having said that, I am not the first
Christian convert after St. Paul's dramatic conversion on the road

---

[3]See Donald Robinson, *Faith's Framework: The Structure of New Testament Theology* (Sutherland:
Albatross, 1985), chap. 2, "The 'Gospel' and the 'Apostle.'"

to Damascus. There is a great cloud of witnesses, past and present. *The witness of Christian thought* is another significant part of doing theology. We should learn from others, especially from their engagement with Scripture and their attempts to apply it to life's circumstances. Speaking of life's circumstances introduces a third vital element in the work of theology—what I like to term *the world of human predicament*. In biblical terms we live outside of Eden in the midst of the great rupture. We also live between the cross and the coming again of Christ. Classically put, we wrestle against the world, the flesh, and the devil. We are not yet in the world to come. Theology ought not to be left in some ethereal world like Platonic ideals. Heaven and earth need to connect. Making that connection is the *work of wisdom*. Wisdom is that activity, predicated on the fear of the Lord (Prov. 1:7), which brings the word of revelation, the witness of Christian thought, and the world of human predicament together in meaningful and practical relation.

The title of the book is *Engaging with the Spirit: Real Questions, Practical Answers*. The questions are both crucial and real. People ask them. In fact, one of them in particular, blasphemy against the Spirit, has been discussed from the earliest centuries of Christianity. And our answers ought to affect the practice of the Christian life, whether individual or corporate. As the wise say, theology without application is abortion.

chapter one

WHAT IS BLASPHEMY AGAINST
THE HOLY SPIRIT?

I RECALL AS A YOUNG theological student doing pastoral visitation on Friday afternoons. One person on whom I called was very uneasy at my presence. She had been trained at a sister institution to my own theological college and ordained as a deaconess. She ministered until one day she was so angry with God—she did not tell me why—that she cursed him. Having done so, she was convinced that she had committed the blasphemy against the Holy Spirit and had fallen irrevocably from God's favor. She was now eternally damned. She left her ministry and her church and had lived in misery over the years since. The question of whether we have blasphemed against the Holy Spirit and thus have committed the unpardonable sin troubles many.

Sometimes preachers and writers discuss the question in ways that make this anxiety, especially for young Christians, very understandable. For example, Edwin H. Palmer writes:

> Every sin and blasphemy may be forgiven men, but the blasphemy against the Spirit shall not be forgiven (Mt. 12:31). If any reader of these lines commits this sin, he can never be saved. He will never have a second chance. He may read the Bible or hear the gospel

preached, but entrance to heaven is eternally closed to him. It is too late. God will never pardon. The whole church may pray for him, but it will never help because he has sinned a sin unto death (1 John 5:16). As a matter of fact, the church should not even pray for such a person (1 John 5:16).[1]

Given such forceful language, the question we are addressing then is pastorally a very sensitive one. It needs careful handling. How shall we proceed?

We will look at what has been said about this sin in past times and also some suggestions found in the present. We next turn to the biblical testimony. In doing theology the pastor or theologian ought never to bind the consciences of others with less than the Word of God responsibly interpreted, taught, and applied. There is a moral dimension to doing theology. After that I will offer a theological reflection before concluding the chapter.

BLASPHEMY AGAINST THE SPIRIT: SOME PAST AND PRESENT PERSPECTIVES

According to Bruce Demarest, generally speaking, the term *blasphemy* "connotes a word or deed that directs insolence to the character of God, Christian truth or sacred things."[2] However, with regard to the Holy Spirit in particular, Augustine thought that the biblical texts concerning the blasphemy against the Spirit raise "one of the greatest difficulties for theological understanding" to be found in Holy Scripture.[3] Each of the Synoptic Gospels makes reference to this sin. In broad terms, blasphemy against the Son of Man may find forgiveness in this life (cf. Matt. 12:31; Mark 3:28; Luke 12:10), but blasphemy against the Holy Spirit finds forgiveness neither in this life nor in the life to come (cf. Matt. 12:32; Mark 3:29; Luke 12:10). It is an eternal sin. Hence it has become known as the unpardonable sin. Some other biblical texts have also been identified as describing unpardonable sins, if not the same one on view in the Gospels. These texts include the warning passages found

---

[1] Edwin H. Palmer, *The Holy Spirit*, rev. ed. (Philadelphia: Presbyterian and Reformed, 1971), 165.
[2] B. Demarest, 'Blasphemy,' *NDOT*, entry on "Blasphemy," *EIRC*.
[3] Augustine, *"Sermo 71: De verbis Evangelii Matthaei (XII 32),"* in Michael Welker, trans. John F. Hoffmeyer, *God the Spirit* (Minneapolis: Fortress, 1994), 214.

in Hebrews 6:4–8 and 10:26–31, which speak of falling away and "sinning deliberately after receiving the knowledge of the truth." Also 1 John 5:16 is adduced by some as further evidence of an unpardonable sin ("sin that leads to death"). References to this kind of sin, when read in the Gospels (or Epistles), have made many a sensitive Christian conscience very alarmed. What then is on view in these accounts, according to church leaders and theologians past and present?

A Sin No Longer Possible

One view, championed by some major figures in the early church, argues that since Jesus no longer walks the earth performing exorcisms, this sin is no longer a possibility. It was only possible before the ascension of Christ, but not after. Chrysostom (c. 347–407) and Jerome (c. 342–420) held this position.[4] This ancient line of interpretation has some contemporary advocates. A dispensational variation of this view is that the blasphemy against the Holy Spirit was a specific sin of unbelieving Israel in the time of Jesus. Arnold G. Fruchtenbaum, for example, argues that: "The unpardonable sin, or the blasphemy of the Holy Spirit, is defined, therefore, as the national rejection by Israel of the messiahship of Jesus was while He was present and claiming He was demon-possessed"[5] (the strange syntax is in the original). He claims further that: "The consequence for Israel is the coming destruction of Jerusalem and the temple, fulfilled in A.D. 70" (the fall of Jerusalem to the Romans).[6]

A Sin Still Possible but Not in Every Aspect

According to Reformed theologian Louis Berkhof, there are a number of New Testament texts that are thought to refer to the unpardonable sin "or blasphemy against the Holy Spirit. The Savior

---

[4]Louis Berkhof, *Systematic Theology* (London: Banner of Truth Trust, 1969), 252. Not all the Fathers, of course, took this line. Gregory of Nyssa (c. 330–c. 395) thought that his contemporaries the Macedonians, who denied both worship of the Spirit and that the Spirit possesses divine glory, were in danger of the blasphemy against the Spirit, *On the Holy Spirit: Against the Macedonians*, http://www.newadvent.org/fathers (accessed August 29, 2005).

[5]Arnold G. Fruchtenbaum, "Israelology, Doctrine of," ed. Mal Couch, *Dictionary of Premillennial Theology: A Practical Guide to the People, Viewpoints, and History of Prophetic Studies* (Grand Rapids, MI: Kregel, 1996), 198.

[6]Ibid.

speaks of it explicitly in Matthew 12:31–32 and parallel passages; and it is generally thought that Hebrews 6:4–6; 10:26, 27 and John 5:16 [sic., actually 1 John 5:16] also refer to this sin."[7] After briefly examining the relevant New Testament texts, he concludes:

> It is evidently a sin committed during the present life, which makes conversion and pardon impossible. The sin consists in the conscious, malicious, and willful rejection and slandering, against evidence and conviction, of the testimony of the Holy Spirit respecting the grace of God in Christ, attributing it out of hatred and enmity to the prince of darkness.[8]

He maintains that the Gospel texts about sinning against the Holy Spirit and Hebrews 6:4–6 and 10:26, 27, 29 and 1 John 5:16 are referring to the same sin. However, he offers a qualification; namely, that the warning passage in Hebrews 6 "speaks of a specific form of this sin, such as could only occur in the apostolic age, when the Spirit revealed itself [sic.] in extraordinary gifts and powers."[9]

A Sin Still Possible

Edwin H. Palmer's approach largely comports with that of Berkhof's own. However, there is a major difference. Palmer, writing also as a Reformed theologian, sees Hebrews 6:4–5 as the grid through which to understand blasphemy against the Holy Spirit. He carefully distinguishes what is not the unpardonable sin: "Final Unbelief," "Denial of Christ," "Denial of the Deity of the Holy Spirit," "Grieving the Holy Spirit," and "Falling Away of the Saved."[10] The last sin on the list is impossible, since in his Calvinist theology the saints persevere to the end. Consequently, the blasphemer against the Spirit is not a Christian, but someone who has experienced the Holy Spirit's working "though in a non-saving way." This blasphemer has been enlightened (received a knowledge of the truth, as in Heb. 10:26). His example is Judas. The blasphemer has tasted of the heavenly gift (the gift is the life and work of Christ). Such persons have

---

[7]Berkhof, *Theology*, 252.
[8]Ibid., 253.
[9]Ibid., 254. Berkhof appears to be a cessationist as far as the charismata are concerned. Miracles as described in the pages of the New Testament are not part of the present church's story.
[10]Palmer, *Spirit*. For the substance of this paragraph I am indebted to Palmer's work, 165–71.

partaken of the Holy Spirit, but not in the sense that the Spirit has indwelt them. Rather they have experienced the Spirit's influence. His examples are Balaam, Saul, and Judas. This person has tasted the Word of God. Affection for the Word has been shown, yet that Word has not been embraced (e.g., King Herod). The powers of the age to come have been tasted (miracles have been seen as in Heb. 2:4) and yet these persons have fallen away and denounced Christ willfully (Heb. 10:26).

So, unlike Berkhof, Palmer argues that Hebrews 6 and 10 apply as they stand to today's world. (Palmer links Hebrews 6 and 10 together.) He writes:

> This same sin can happen today as much as it did in biblical times. Although the age of miracles has passed, it is possible for modern man, enlightened by the Spirit of God and tasting that the Word of God is good, to rebel against Christ openly, brazenly and without remorse. This is especially true of those reared in orthodox Christian homes and churches where they have heard the gospel fully, plainly and properly over the years. It is possible for them to be warmed to the clear presentation of the gospel and then willfully, hatefully and openly to renounce Christ completely.[11]

Like Berkhof, Palmer is convinced that the elect child of God cannot commit such a sin. The biblical warnings about it then are addressed to the outsider.[12]

Arminian theologian J. Kenneth Grider is not convinced that 1 John 5:16 is relevant to the discussion. According to him, the Johannine text refers "to a sin which carries the death penalty in civil law."[13] The church is not necessarily to pray for someone so condemned, if such praying aims at the alleviation of the penalty. How Grider arrives at this view is not clear. As for the Gospel texts, these refer to that sin where a person knowing full well that the Holy Spirit is the source of Jesus' ministry attributes it to an evil

---

[11]Ibid., 171.

[12]For a different view with regard to the Hebrews passages, see Mark E. Biddle, who argues that the passages are speaking about believers, *Missing the Mark: Sin and Its Consequences in Biblical Theology* (Nashville, TN: Abingdon, 2005), 29–30.

[13]J. Kenneth Grider, "Unpardonable Sin," ed. Richard S. Taylor, *Beacon Dictionary of Theology* (Kansas City, MO: Beacon Hill, 1983), 537. All contributions to this valuable resource are written from an Arminian stance.

spirit instead. Grider's Arminianism becomes especially apparent
when he suggests that such a sin "is unpardonable because the
person himself sets himself into this kind of stance and *will not let
God transform his mind and forgive him*. It is therefore unpardonable more from man's standpoint than from God's—for we read
elsewhere in Scripture that God will graciously forgive anyone who
asks for pardon."[14] Miroslav Volf argues similarly: "*There are no
unforgivable sins. There are no unforgivable people.*"[15] A reviewer
of Volf's book on grace, John Wilson, rightly raises the question:
"What about the sin against the Holy Spirit?" Volf's answer is:
"That is the sin of closing oneself off to the One through whom God
forgives all people and all sins."[16] However, this approach seems to
turn the blasphemy against the Holy Spirit into the sin of unasked-
for forgiveness. Also writing from an Arminian stance, John B.
Nielson maintains that the blasphemy against the Holy Spirit is not
to be confused with the sin leading to death of 1 John 5:16, nor with
the apostasy referred to in Hebrews 6 and 10. He argues: "Jesus
limits the unpardonable sin to the intention of attributing the work
of the Holy Spirit done in Christ to the power of Satan."[17]

As can be seen in this brief survey of opinion past and present,
there is much variety in interpretation. What then are we to make
of the biblical testimony?

BIBLICAL TESTIMONY

In Matthew, Jesus warns the Pharisees about this sin. He has just
cast out a demon. But their response is to attribute the exorcism to
Beelzebub, the prince of demons. In the Matthean account Jesus
counters: "But if it is by the Spirit of God that I cast out demons,
then the kingdom of God has come upon you" (Matt. 12:28).[18]

---

[14]Ibid. (my emphasis). Grider's commitment to libertarian freewill is evident here, but it is ques-
tionable whether he has done justice to the thrust of relevant Gospel texts.
[15]Quoted in Miroslav Volf, *Free of Charge: Giving and Forgiving in a Culture Stripped of Grace*,
reviewed by John Wilson in *Christianity Today*, June 2006, 61 (original emphases).
[16]Ibid.
[17]John B. Nielson, "Blasphemy," in *Beacon Dictionary of Theology*, 79.
[18]With regard to Matt. 12:28, Max Turner points out: "This is striking, as no available Jewish
sources directly connect exorcisms with the Spirit nor do they explicitly interpret exorcisms as
evidence of the arrival of the kingdom," *The Holy Spirit and Spiritual Gifts Then and Now*, rev.
ed. (Carlisle: Paternoster, 1999), 32.

The pericope ends with Jesus issuing a generalized warning which is addressed to "whoever [*hos*] speaks a word . . . against [*kata*] the Holy Spirit" (Matt. 12:32). In Luke, Jesus warns the disciples—not the Pharisees this time—about the sin. The warning is applicable to "the one who blasphemes against the Holy Spirit" (Luke 12:10).[19] Mark does not name the Pharisees but refers to "the scribes who came down from Jerusalem" (Mark 3:22). The Markan account is more specific: "but whoever blasphemes against the Holy Spirit never has forgiveness, but is guilty of an eternal sin—for they had said, 'He has an unclean spirit'" (Mark 3:29–30). For readers who are also preachers the differences are no surprise. The same teaching may allow multiple applications depending upon audience and occasion. Likewise here. There is no need to postulate one of these accounts as more primitive than the other or merely a reworking of the other by a redactor. What is common to the accounts is the rejection of Jesus and its consequences. But what does that rejection of Jesus entail exactly?

A common interpretation has been to suggest that on view in these accounts, whether addressed to Pharisees (outsiders) or scribes (outsiders, perhaps also Pharisees) or disciples (insiders), is unbelief or impenitence. In the patristic era Augustine held this view, as did Melanchthon in the Reformation period.[20] The unbelief reading has had, then, a long history in the church. But is this interpretation too general in attempting to cover outsiders and insiders?

Another interpretation is that the sin refers to a specific deed: knowingly attributing Jesus' miraculous works to Satan rather than to the Spirit of God. In contrast to blasphemy against the Son of Man (Jesus), which may flow from ignorance, this sin is malicious in intent. Good has become evil. Louis Berkhof championed this reading, as we have seen. The person who so describes Jesus is so locked into the abyss that the sin is unpardonable, either because God will not forgive such a blasphemy, or because such a person will never embrace the proffered grace of God.

---

[19]Turner convincingly argues that the parallel to Matt. 12:28 found in Luke 11:20 which speaks of "the finger of God" rather than "the Spirit of God" probably has the Spirit in view and is using an image drawn from the Old Testament, ibid., 33.
[20]Berkhof, *Theology*, 253.

A still further interpretation maintains that Luke 12:10 has the specific sin of apostasy in mind. Unlike the Matthean and Markan accounts, this text is unconnected to the Beelzebub controversy.[21] Jesus addresses disciples (his *philoi*, "friends") in this context. The backdrop is a warning concerning the Pharisees: "Beware of the leaven of the Pharisees" (Luke 12:1). (Is this leaven their false view of Jesus?) Then Jesus warns the disciples still further about not fearing those who can kill only the body as opposed to the soul (Luke 12:4–7). Against that background the disciples are encouraged to acknowledge Christ before others in contrast to denying him (Luke 12:8–9). Speaking a word against the Son of Man will be forgiven, but blasphemy against the Spirit will not be (Luke 12:10). Next, Jesus speaks of the disciples having to face the authorities for their faith, but the Holy Spirit will teach them what to say (Luke 12:11–12). Because of these elements in the context some have suggested that for Luke apostasy under hostile pressure is tantamount to blasphemy against the Holy Spirit.[22] However, it is difficult to account for Jesus' intercession for Peter, Peter's denial of Christ, and Peter's subsequent reinstatement on this view (cf. Luke 12:8–12; 22:54–62; 22:31–34).

Yet another possibility has been suggested by H. A. G. Blocher. He argues that Christ was incognito in his earthly ministry. Consequently, failing to recognize his glory did not merit the culpability it would attract subsequent to his glorification. However, to ascribe the Spirit's works to demonic power is fatal. The Spirit is the one who draws us to Christ without whom there is no forgiveness. Blocher contends: "To oppose the Spirit, refusing to be convinced by his witness to the only way of salvation, it [sic., is?] to deny oneself access to salvation."[23]

Still another suggestion, that of Graeme Twelftree, is that the incident narrated in Acts 5:1–5 concerning Ananias and Sapphira is a Lukan example of the unpardonable sin or blasphemy against the

---

[21]Walter L. Liefeld, "Luke," *EBC*, comment on Luke 12:11–12: "This separation [from the Beelzebub controversy] not only raises questions of tradition history beyond the scope of this commentary but also makes exegesis of the passage difficult."

[22]See, for example, W. H. C. Frend, *Martyrdom and Persecution in the Early Church* (Oxford: Oxford University Press, 1965), 79, and A. A. Trites, *The New Testament Concept of Witness* (Cambridge: Cambridge University Press, 1977), 182.

[23]H. A. G. Blocher, "Sin," *NDBT*, *EIRC*. This view was also championed earlier by G. C. Berkouwer, and Blocher acknowledges his debt.

Spirit.[24] The suggestion is an interesting one. A specific deed is on view in the text. Ananias and Sapphira sin against the Holy Spirit by misrepresenting how much they had donated to the needs of the community. However, the sin is never described *in situ* as blasphemy; rather it is described as a lie. Furthermore, there is no hint in the text that this is an unpardonable sin. Luke has a blasphemy against the Holy Spirit story in his Gospel, so that category was known to the writer. But he does not employ it in Acts. A better analogue perhaps is the Corinthian situation, where some had died because of their abuse of the Lord's Supper (1 Cor. 11:30). There are sins, it seems, that are worthy of removal of the perpetrator from this life. This does not mean necessarily that such persons are lost for ever.

One further suggestion is worth noting. Michael Welker contends that the blasphemy against the Spirit is nothing less than "disregarding God's already experienced intervention [through Jesus] in the world of human beings. It means, *contrary to better experience*, not taking either God or oneself and suffering and liberated people seriously—and to do one is always to do the other."[25] The Pharisees disregarded "the undeniable experience of diverse deliverance out of distress from which there is, by human standards, no escape."[26] Jesus' warning then is "directed against those who take the last hope away from others [because the Pharisees and scribes are religious authority figures their judgment of Jesus will be listened to by the poor], and who obstruct their own access to a last hope."[27]

A verbal blasphemy against the Son of Man may be forgiven. Paul, in his former life as Saul of Tarsus, is a case in point. Paul describes himself to Timothy as "a blasphemer, persecutor, and insolent opponent" of the faith (1 Tim. 1:13). However, he also writes of his acting "ignorantly in unbelief." As history shows, his was not a fixed, unalterable hostility to Christ. The grace of God transformed him (*hyperpleonasen*, grace "overflowed," 1 Tim. 1:14). But the settled rejection of the Spirit's testimony to and through Jesus is

---

[24]G. H. Twelftree, "2. Blasphemy against the Holy Spirit," *DJG*.
[25]Welker, *Spirit*, 219 (original emphasis).
[26]Ibid., 218.
[27]Ibid., cf. 212, 218. As Welker suggests: ". . . the judgment of religious experts carries a lot of weight."

eternally freighted in its consequences.[28] What is clear in the various
Gospels' accounts is the nexus between Christology and pneumatology in blasphemy against the Holy Spirit. But as we have seen,
the Ananias and Sapphira story in Acts 5:1–6 does not exhibit such
a nexus. Moreover, there is no suggestion in the text that their sin
resulted in more than physical death. However, there may well be
other sins—in addition to blasphemy against the Holy Spirit—that
are unpardonable ones. For example, 1 John 5:16–17 may refer
to such a sin. However, there is no hint in the text that either
Christology or pneumatology or both are in mind. So although
some (e.g., Edwin Palmer and Louis Berkhof) would like to link the
Gospel texts with 1 John 5:16, it is too much of a stretch to do so
(e.g., so Grudem rightly argues).[29]

My own view is that Jesus warned the Pharisees and scribes
that they were in danger of committing the sin, not that they had
committed it (*enochos* may be translated "liable").[30] They had
attributed Jesus' work to the devil, but that mere attribution was
dangerous, not yet deadly. More than a specific deed appears to be
in mind as Jesus spoke. Persistent willful rejection of Jesus and thus
of the Spirit's revelatory work through him, together with depicting
such work as an evil, results in no forgiveness in this life, or in the
world to come. O. E. Evans comments:

> To call good evil in this way is to deliberately pervert all moral
> values, and to persist in such an attitude can only result in a pro-
> gressive blunting of moral sensibility, the ultimate conclusion of
> which will be to become so hardened in sin as to lose for ever the
> capacity to recognize the value of goodness and to be attracted to
> it. To reach such a state is to be incapable of repentance; the sinner

---

[28]I cannot subscribe to Donald G. Bloesch's view that "[t]he sin against the Holy Spirit cannot
be forgiven, but it can be changed—from a curse to a blessing, or from an unmitigated curse
to a curse with a blessing," *The Last Things: Resurrection, Judgment, Glory* (Downers Grove,
IL: InterVarsity, 2004), 218. He does not preclude the possibility of a passageway from hell to
heaven as he believes in "Grace Invincible," ibid., 226, 232. Too much Barth, too little Bible, in
my view.

[29]Wayne Grudem, *Systematic Theology: An Introduction to Biblical Doctrine* (Leicester: Inter-
Varsity Press; Grand Rapids, MI: Zondervan, 1994), 509. Although Grudem is indebted to
Berkhof at a number of points, he does not follow Berkhof in including 1 John 5:16 in discussing
the Gospel accounts of blasphemy against the Spirit. With regard to his indebtedness, the only
theologian referred to in his footnotes as well as in the main text is Berkhof.

[30]See Robert A. Guelich, *Mark 1 – 8:26*, WBC 34A, comment on Mark 3:22–30: "In so doing,
Mark clarifies the seriousness of the charge in 3:22a through the warning of 3:28–29, but stops
short of pronouncing final judgment on the scribes."

has shut himself out, irrevocably and eternally, from the forgiving mercy of God.[31]

Even so, the very fact that Jesus reasons with his opponents suggests that they had not yet crossed the line of no return. In other words, simply saying "He has an unclean spirit" or even temporarily thinking it is not sufficient to have committed this calamitous sin.[32]

In sum, the blasphemy against the Spirit is that self-righteous persistent refusal to embrace the offer of salvation in Christ: his ministry of restoring his Father's broken creation. It is to set one's face against the Spirit's testimony to Christ as the Son of Man with the authority to forgive sins. The problem is the human heart settled in opposition to God. Without repentance there is no forgiveness.[33] As Mark E. Biddle suggests: "Thus, all three traditions [the Synoptic Gospels] regard failure to recognize Jesus as the ultimate sin."[34] Of course, the person who persists in the view that Jesus was an agent of the prince of darkness would exemplify such a sin.

THEOLOGICAL REFLECTION

As we wrestle not only with the meaning of the biblical texts but also with their import for Christian life and ministry today, we shall address two issues: the role of blasphemy against the Spirit texts and related ones with regard to the sensitive Christian and the pastoral care of the anxious believer.

The Role of Such Warnings

I remember being told as a young Christian that if I was worried that I had blasphemed the Holy Spirit and committed the unpardonable sin, then most probably I had not. I have heard and read that

---

[31]Quoted with approval by Charles H. H. Scobie, *The Ways of Our God: An Approach to Biblical Theology* (Grand Rapids, MI; Cambridge: Eerdmans, 2003), 295–96.

[32]See G. Burge, "Sin, Unpardonable," *EDT*, 1017: "The meaning of this sin in Christian thought is best viewed as a total and persistent denial of the presence of God in Christ. It reflects a complete recalcitrance of heart. Rather than a particular act, it is a disposition of the will."

[33]John Paul II rightly argues in his treatment of the sin against the Holy Spirit: "If Jesus says that blasphemy against the Holy Spirit cannot be forgiven either in this life or in the next, it is because this *'non-forgiveness'* is linked, as to its cause, to *'non-repentance,'* in other words to the radical refusal to be converted," *The Holy Spirit in the Life of the Church and the World: Dominum et Vivificantem*, trans. Vatican (Boston: Pauline Books and Media, 1986), 79 (original emphases).

[34]Biddle, *Missing*, 146, fn. 20.

advice many times since. As for those Christians fearful that they have committed the sin of blasphemy against the Holy Spirit—and I have met some who have been—there is great wisdom in the old advice that those troubled about committing this sin are the least likely to have committed it. For example, Louis Berkhof, writing as a Calvinist theologian, argues: "We may be reasonably sure that they who fear that they have committed it and worry about this, and who desire the prayers of others for them, have not committed it."[35] And J. Kenneth Grider, writing as an Arminian theologian, counsels: "The most important thing to remember about the unpardonable sin is that anyone who fears that he has committed it, and is concerned about the matter, hasn't."[36] If that is so, then what role do such warnings—whether found in the Gospels or Hebrews or 1 John—play in the Christian's life?

Before we address the question we need to note that there is a long-standing difference of theological opinion amongst Christians with a high view of biblical authority as to whether a genuine Christian could ever commit such sins and therefore be irredeemably lost. On the one hand, Calvinist theologians argue for the eternal security of the saints, for such is God's sovereign grace. On the other hand, Arminian theologians believe that genuine believers may be lost, for such is the reality of human free will. In the light of the debate, Scot McKnight wisely argues that "because apostasy is disputed among theologians, it must be recognized that one's overall hermeneutic and theology (including one's general philosophical orientation) shapes how one reads texts dealing with apostasy."[37] My own approach assumes that the genuine believer cannot be plucked out of the Father's hand—as Jesus taught (John 10:29).[38]

Let me approach the question in a somewhat oblique fashion,

---

[35]Berkhof, *Theology*, 254.

[36]Grider, "Unpardonable Sin," 537.

[37]Scot McKnight, "Apostasy," ed. Kevin J. Vanhoozer, *Dictionary for Theological Interpretation of the Bible* (London: SPCK; Grand Rapids, MI: Baker Academic, 2005), 59. McKnight includes the blasphemy against the Spirit in his discussion.

[38]Scot McKnight takes a very different approach, ibid. 60: "*Pastorally, apostasy needs to be muted by the sufficiency of God's work in Christ and through his Spirit while it is held up as a rare, but real, possibility*" (original emphasis). In my view, the warning passages in Hebrews, in the writer's own mind, are not in the first instance true to his knowledge of his Christian readers (Heb. 6:9–12). So why write them? Probably because the writer also knows that he could be wrong about some of them and that congregations are mixed multitudes.

but I hope in a way that offers a useful analogy. In Acts 27 we find a graphic account of a shipwreck that Paul experienced on his way to Rome to appear before Caesar. He is under guard. Because of the time of year, Paul warned the centurion that if they put to sea then lives would be lost (Acts 27:9–10). His advice was ignored by both the centurion and the ship's owner. The ship meets a dreadful storm (Acts 27:13–20). A night came in which the situation seemed hopeless, but Paul had a revelation from God to share. An angel had told him that very night: "God has granted you all those who sail with you" (Acts 27:24). But the storm still raged and some of the crew decided to save themselves by using the ship's boat to make for shore. However, Paul warned: "Unless these men stay in the ship, you cannot be saved" (Acts 27:27–32). The centurion believed Paul. All stayed aboard. Eventually the ship was lost, but all on board were saved just as the angel had said (Acts 27:39–44).

How is this story relevant to our question? God is a God not only of ends (objectives) but of means (processes to get there). Paul had the Word of God to assure him that all would be saved and yet he issued a warning. That warning becomes the very means by which the divine promise comes to pass. Let me suggest that the warning passages in the New Testament function like that in the genuine Christian's life. It is the genuine Christian who is troubled by them. The outsider is not. Sadly the warning passages about the blasphemy of the Spirit—whether heard preached or read in Scripture—then function as instruments of judgment for those who want to call good evil and who persistently dismiss Jesus' kingdom claim on their lives. This is especially true of those characterized by that settled opposition to God and his Christ that I have argued is the blasphemy against the Spirit.

Pastoral Care

How then is the Christian troubled by such passages to be helped pastorally? Clarification may be the first need. Blaspheming the Spirit is not backsliding. According to Scot McKnight: "Many theologians distinguish between 'backsliding' (forgivable lapses of the believer) and 'apostasy' (permanent, unforgivable lapses)."[39] The distinction is sound. Christians do sin. John's first letter makes that plain (1 John 1:9). A Christian who has been drifting away from Christ and is now troubled by that fact and is wondering if there is a way back needs to be assured that there is. Blaspheming against the Spirit is not simply to experience doubt.

In fact, there are different kinds of doubting in the New Testament. John the Baptist had doubts about whether Jesus was the coming one after all. He sent disciples to put the question to Jesus (Matt. 11:2–3). Jesus answered them, but at no stage criticized the Baptist for asking the question. Instead he praised John for his part in the unfolding story of salvation history. According to Jesus, the Baptist is the promised Elijah figure of Old Testament hope, "more than a prophet" and "among those born of women there has arisen no one greater than John the Baptist" (Matt. 11:9–14). But with Thomas, Jesus responds to his doubts with a rebuke. Thomas is to stop his unbelief and believe: "Do not disbelieve, but believe" (John 20:27). There is then doubt that arises from perplexity as in the case of John the Baptist, and then there is the doubt of unbelief as exhibited by Thomas. In both cases, Christology is the answer. Back to Christ, his person, words, and works.

Moreover, blasphemy against the Holy Spirit is not being angry with God. There are many laments in Scripture, especially in the Psalms. There is a common acronym used to sum up prayer found in evangelical circles: ACTS. "A" stands for adoration (e.g., Psalm 150). "C" is confession (Psalm 32). "T" is thanksgiving (Psalm 118). And "S" is supplication (Psalm 116). Each of these practices has good biblical warrant. What is missing is *the problem of pain.* What are God's children to say to God when the divine government of the world seems derelict? How are they to relate to God when needless tragedy is experienced? I recall a friend who, while training to be a missionary, accidentally backed over his infant who was crawling on the lawn. Each parent thought that the other was watching out. ACTS seems most inadequate in such circumstances. But Scripture provides a language in the Psalms not only for our joys, sorrow over

---

[39]Ibid., 58.

our sins, delight in God, and burden for others. The Bible also gives us the language of *lament* (Psalm 22). Lamenting to God, whether in anguish or anger, is not to commit the blasphemy against the Holy Spirit. It is to be real. I suspect God prefers to be related to in anger by his children than not to be related to at all. ACTS needs to be LACTS to do justice to the pastoral wisdom of Scripture.

Anxious Christians who are wondering whether they have committed the unpardonable sin by blaspheming against the Spirit need to be helped to name what they are experiencing and pastored accordingly. They also need to know what the blasphemy against the Holy Spirit is about; namely, a settled, persistent refusal to give Jesus his due and with it failing to acknowledge the truth of the Holy Spirit's testimony to God's saving project. And that project is to restore his creation, which centers on the Son of Man. I recall sharing the gospel the best I could with someone who, having heard me out, declared: "Your God is a bastard!" I have prayed for him off and on since. That attitude, unless repented of, will never lead to the Father's house but into a darkness that never ends. The very fact that a person asks anxiously whether they have sinned the unforgivable sin betrays a very different spirit. Hence the long-standing Christian wisdom, already mentioned, that the person who is so troubled is displaying the evidence that such a sin is not true of them.

CONCLUSION

Reading Scripture can be a sobering experience. God is not only love (1 John 4:8). God is also light (1 John 1:5). Scripture not only contains words of incredible invitation, love, and hope (e.g., John 3:16). It also presents warnings of the direst kind (2 Thess. 1:5–10). The blasphemy against the Spirit is found amongst the warnings, and it is a sin that has eternal consequences. Attributing the source of Jesus' healing power to Satan is to slander the Holy Spirit and is symptomatic of an attitude to God which, if settled and never abandoned, leads only into a darkness without end. This sin is against the Holy Spirit. Moreover, there is a nexus between Christology and pneumatology in this regard; Jesus' ministry is deeply disvalued in this sin. In my view, this is a sin of the outsider, not the insider. Any Christian disturbed as to whether they have committed this sin needs to be encouraged to think that they have not. Rather, such warnings, I suggest, are used by the Spirit to recover the drifting Christian and to encourage perseverance in the faith. The tender Christian conscience is a sign of hope, not evidence for despair.

chapter two

HOW MAY WE RESIST
THE HOLY SPIRIT?

THERE ARE A NUMBER OF sins that are specifically identified in Scripture as sins against the Holy Spirit. In the last chapter we examined blasphemy against the Spirit as delineated in the Gospels. In subsequent chapters we shall explore the Bible's teaching of quenching the Spirit and grieving the Spirit.[1] In this discussion we turn to the book of Acts and one of the great speeches found there. In his speech in Acts 7, Stephen, the first Christian martyr, declares to his hearers: "You stiff-necked people, uncircumcised in heart and ears, you always resist the Holy Spirit" (Acts 7:51). Unlike the blasphemy against the Holy Spirit that appears to be the sin of individuals, Stephen identifies this sin as the sin of a people over time.

We will first examine some past and present understandings of what resisting the Spirit means. Next we will explore Stephen's famous and courageous "How not to win friends and influence people" speech that led to his death. A theological reflection follows, which attempts to bring the text and today together through the medium of faithful theological reflection. It has been said that

---

[1]A further sin that will not be examined in this book is that of outraging (*enybrizō*, outrage or insult) the Spirit of grace, referred to in Heb. 10:29.

theology without application is an abortion. But application must be grounded in a theologically responsible reading of Scripture as special revelation from God. Otherwise, the conscience of a Christian may be bound by mere human opinion in matters concerning God and human beings.

RESISTING THE HOLY SPIRIT:
SOME PAST AND PRESENT PERSPECTIVES

Although there is only one reference to resisting the Holy Spirit per se in Scripture (Acts 7:51), the idea has been the subject of much controversy since the early part of the seventeenth century. If the Holy Spirit may be resisted, does that entail that the grace of God may be resisted? A group of theologians in the Netherlands thought so. These theologians were disciples of Jacobus Arminius (c. 1560–1609) and came to be known as the Remonstrants ("opposers") who dissented from the Calvinistic orthodoxy of their day.[2] They drafted Five Articles (Remonstrance) on the matter in 1610. One of them explicitly refers to resisting the Spirit:

> That this grace of God is the beginning, continuance, and accomplishment of all good, even to the extent that the regenerate man himself, without prevenient or assisting, awakening, following and cooperative grace, can neither think, will, nor do good, nor withstand any temptation to evil; so that all good deeds or movements that can be conceived must be ascribed to the grace of God in Christ. *But with respect to the mode of the operation of this grace, it is not irresistible, since it is written concerning many, that they have resisted the Holy Spirit (Acts 7, and elsewhere in many places).*[3]

Thus Article 4 of the Remonstrance thematizes the notion of resisting the Holy Spirit and connects it with resisting God's grace and Acts 7 in particular.

A synod was convened at Dordt in 1618 and 1619 to address the controversy. The Remonstrants were defeated and counter can-

---

[2]For a good discussion of both the Calvinist and Arminian views, see Bruce Demarest, *The Cross and Salvation* (Wheaton, IL: Crossway Books, 1997), 55–59, 204–29. Note *prevenient* means "goes before."

[3]Dennis Bratcher, ed., *The Five Articles of the Remonstrants* (1610), http://www.crivoice.org/creedremonstrants.html (accessed May 28, 2006), adapted from Phillip Schaff, *The Creeds of Christendom*, vol. 3 (Grand Rapids, MI: Baker Books, 1996), 545ff. (emphasis mine).

ons promulgated. The Remonstrants' position on resisting the Spirit was formally rejected:

Rejections
The true doctrine having been explained, the Synod rejects the errors of those:

> Who teach: that . . . man may yet so resist God and the Holy Spirit, when God intends man's regeneration and wills to regenerate him, and indeed that man often does so resist that he prevents entirely his regeneration, and that it therefore remains in man's power to be regenerated or not.[4]

In Dordt's view, God's grace is irresistible with regard to the elect. Although the controversy was based in the Netherlands, delegates came to Dordt from numerous places in the Protestant world, including Great Britain, Switzerland, and France.

This Calvinistic notion of irresistible grace constitutes the fourth element in that famous piece of theological horticulture known as TULIP: Total Depravity, Unconditional Election (God's eternal choice not our own), Limited Atonement (Christ died for the sins of the elect only), Irresistible Grace (the Holy Spirit cannot be defeated), and Perseverance of the Saints (eternal security). The Arminian theology that was refined in subsequent history affirmed Total Depravity (but offset by prevenient grace), Conditional Election (based on foreseen faith), Universal Atonement (Christ died for all without exception), Resistible Grace, and that Saints may fall away from the Faith and in fact some do so without recovery.

Debate continues amongst those holding a high view of biblical authority on the subject of whether the Spirit or grace may be resisted. As Alistair Mason suggests: "There are . . . still Calvinists eager for battle. Who, they ask, is really content with universal *non-efficacious* atonement and universal *resistible* grace?"[5] Contemporary Arminian theologians, however, take a very different view. For example, Fritz Guy contends:

---

[4]"Of the Corruption of Man, His Conversion to God, and the Manner Thereof," *The Canons of Dordt—Text, Rejection VIII*, http://mb-soft.com/believe/txh/dort1.htm (accessed May 28, 2006).
[5]Alistair Mason, "Arminianism" in Adrian Hastings, Alistair Mason, and Hugh Pyper, eds., *The Oxford Companion to Christian Thought* (Oxford: Oxford University Press, 2000), 41 (original emphasis).

For grace is never, strictly speaking, "irresistible." Indeed, the term "irresistible grace" looks suspiciously like an oxymoron, like "married bachelor" or "square circle" or "causally determined free action." For grace is the offer of a gift, not the imposition of another's will; and it is the nature of a gift that it can be rejected. It is the nature of love that it can be ignored or spurned. That is why it made logical (although not perhaps diplomatic) sense for Stephen to say to the leaders of the religious establishment in Jerusalem, "You always resist the Holy Spirit" (Acts 7:51).[6]

The question is whether the key text in Acts 7:51 that refers to resisting the Spirit has anything to do with this long-standing controversy at all. After all, there is no mention of grace in the text, nor arguably is the concept there under another guise. To answer that question we must next attend to the biblical text.

BIBLICAL TESTIMONY

Stephen is one of "Three Big Men" that Acts 6:8–9:31 keeps in focus.[7] The other two are Philip and Saul of Tarsus, who becomes Paul the apostle. Stephen's story is the first to appear at length in the narrative. In fact, Stephen's speech before the Jewish council in Acts 7 is the longest in Acts and, as noted previously, contains the one explicit reference to resisting the Holy Spirit in Scripture (Acts 7:51). The word for resist is *antipiptein*, meaning "to strive against" or "to resist."[8] Like other narratives in Acts, we are not dealing with simple reportage. Rather Acts is carefully written to persuade the reader through what Beverly Roberts Gaventa describes as "theological narrative."[9] Stephen's speech is theologically richly laden. I shall explore only those aspects of it relevant to understanding what it was to resist the Spirit.

The accusation brought against Stephen echoes the one brought against Jesus: "This man never ceases to speak words

---

[6]Fritz Guy, "The Universality of God's Love," in Clark H. Pinnock, ed., *A Case for Arminianism: The Grace of God, the Will of Man* (Grand Rapids, MI: Zondervan, 1989), 40.
[7]David Wenham and Steve Walton, *Exploring the New Testament, vol. 1, A Guide to the Gospels and Acts* (Downers Grove, IL: InterVarsity, 2001), 273. I would prefer "Three Major Figures."
[8]G. Abbott-Smith, *A Manual Greek Lexicon of the New Testament*, 3rd ed. (Edinburgh: T. and T. Clark, 1968), 42.
[9]Beverly Roberts Gaventa, "The Acts of the Apostles," Wayne A. Meeks, ed., *The HarperCollins Study Bible: New Revised Standard Version with the Apocryphal/Deuterocanonical Books* (London: HarperCollins, 1993), 2056.

against this holy place [the temple] and the law, for we have heard him say that this Jesus of Nazareth will destroy this place and will change the customs that Moses delivered to us" (Acts 6:13; cf. Matt. 26:59–61). The high priest asks Stephen whether the witnesses were speaking correctly (Acts 7:1). Stephen replies by telling the story of God's promises to his people and their historical outworking, going all the way back into the pre-conquest period with Abraham (Acts 7:2–8), then Joseph (Acts 7:9–16), before getting to Moses (Acts 7:17–42). And how did God's Old Testament people treat Moses? They rejected him: "Our fathers refused to obey him, but thrust him aside, and in their hearts they turned to Egypt" (Acts 7:39). The golden calf fiasco was Exhibit A of their rejection of God's appointed leader and prophet (Acts 7:40–42). And so what did God do? He gave them up to their idolatrous folly (Acts 7:42–43).

The speech culminates in Stephen making his own accusation: "You stiff-necked people, uncircumcised in heart and ears, you always resist [*aei*, 'unceasingly,' *antipiptete*, 'resist,' lit. 'fall against,' second person plural indicative active present aspect] the Holy Spirit" (Acts 7:51). In this resistance, his hearers were just like their fathers. So he asks: "Which of the prophets did not your fathers persecute?" (Acts 7:52). In fact, their forebears had killed those who prophesied "the coming of the Righteous One, whom you have now betrayed and murdered" (Acts 7:52). They had received the law but not kept it (Acts 7:53). Stephen does not get to finish his address. Enraged, his hearers rush him, cast him out of the city, then stone him to death (Acts 7:54–59). And as he dies, Stephen sees the glory of God and Jesus standing at God's right hand in heaven acting as his advocate or vindicating judge (Acts 7:55–56). Significantly, the glory of God is seen not in the temple, but where Jesus now is.[10] And like Jesus, Stephen prays that their sin be not held against them (Acts 7:60, cf. Luke 23:34).

Such strong words have been variously interpreted. Charles H. H. Scobie sees in Stephen's address a radical rejection of the

---

[10]A point well made by Michael Griffiths, *Three Men Filled with the Spirit* (London: Overseas Missionary Fellowship, 1970), 48.

temple: "He [Stephen] virtually portrays Solomon's building of the temple as an act of rebellion (Acts 7:47–53). Isa. 66:1–2 is quoted (Acts 7:49–50) as part of the antitemple polemic."[11] On this view those accusing Stephen had been right. This Hellenist was speaking "against this holy place." However, William J. Dumbrell argues that Stephen is not criticizing the temple per se. Rather he is attacking Israel's turning the temple into "a purely human edifice (v. 47)."[12] He maintains that "the problem was not the temple, but Israel's failure to understand the nature of God's presence and the factors that conditioned it. Without such an understanding the temple was simply a human artifact exposed to depredations of history (v. 48)."[13] Dumbrell's argument makes better sense. The narrative speaks of "false witnesses" making these accusations (Acts 7:13).[14]

The question remains as to how Israel had consistently resisted the Spirit. The context suggests that the resistance lay in not heeding and obeying the Word of God in promise, law, and prophet. Moses as a prophet provided Stephen with a paradigm case (cf. v. 17 for "promise"; v. 37 for Moses as "prophet"; v. 42 "the prophets"; v. 48 "the prophet"; and v. 53 "the law"). The Holy Spirit is presented in Acts as the ultimate source of the Word of God both spoken and written (e.g., Acts 1:16 written; 2:4 spoken; 4:25 written; 4:31 spoken; 28:25 written).[15] Moreover, they had rejected "the Righteous One" (Acts 7:52). Furthermore, in rejecting Stephen's words his hearers were guilty of more of the same. He too had the Spirit in his speaking (Acts 6:5, 10). Yet they became enraged at him, killing him as they had killed Jesus.

But why did Stephen's hearers react in such a violent way to his speech? According to David Peterson:

---

[11]Charles H. H. Scobie, The *Ways of Our God: An Approach to Biblical Theology* (Grand Rapids, MI; Cambridge: Eerdmans, 2003), 592.

[12]William J. Dumbrell, *The Search for Order: Biblical Eschatology in Focus* (Eugene, OR: Wipf and Stock, 2001), 228.

[13]Ibid.

[14]As B. L. Backburn points out: "Likewise he was charged with claiming that Jesus would destroy the temple (Acts 6:13–14). While this latter charge might not be entirely accurate, Stephen himself was allegedly critical of the temple (Acts 7:47–50). Against these considerations, however, one should note that Luke represents the charges against Stephen as false (Acts 6:13)," "Stephen," *DLNTD, EIRC.*

[15]I owe this insight to Dr. David Peterson, Principal of Oak Hill College, London.

Those who act in this way show themselves to be spiritually uncircumcised (cf. Lev. 26:41; Deut. 10:16; Jer. 4:4; 6:10) and, therefore, not true Israelites. They demonstrate the need for the sort of forgiveness and transformation of heart by God's Spirit mentioned in Jeremiah 31:31–4 and the related prophecy of Ezekiel 36:26–27.[16]

Moreover, Stephen declares his hearers to be stiff-necked (*sklērotraxēlos*, obstinate, stubborn). Thus he employs standard Old Testament-like prophetic insult.[17] In their obstinacy the hearers were just like that wilderness generation that fell into the idolatry of the golden calf (see Ex. 33:3, 5; 34:9, LXX).

THEOLOGICAL REFLECTION

As we reflect theologically on Stephen's speech we shall consider the challenge of deriving doctrine from narrative; the important distinction in theology between an external and internal call in relation to the gospel; contrasting responses to the Word of God in Acts; and the relationship between Christian boldness, the Spirit, and prayer.

Deriving Doctrine from Narrative

The controversy between Calvinists and Arminians raises the important question of what to do with narrative doctrinally speaking. Do we ignore narrative when building doctrine? Do we use the epistles to build doctrine and narrative for illustrative purposes only? Bernard Ramm, for example, argues:

> To build a theology of the Holy Spirit primarily on the Book of Acts is contrary to the fundamental Protestant principle of interpretation: *Scripture interprets Scripture*. The great theology of the Holy Spirit is clearest in John's Gospel and Paul's letters. Here is where the great doctors of the church have built their doctrine of the Holy Spirit, and rightly so.[18]

Or again, Sinclair Ferguson in his discussion of Acts maintains that "we are to find doctrine that is already formulated elsewhere

---

[16]David Peterson, *Prophecy and Preaching: Acts and the Church Today* (Buxton, Derbyshire: Fellowship of Word and Spirit, 1997), 4.
[17]See Craig S. Keener, *IBBCNT, EIRC*, comment on Acts 7:51.
[18]Bernard Ramm, *Rapping about the Spirit* (Waco, TX: Word, 1974), 113 (original emphasis).

illustrated in the historical narratives."[19] Or is that approach unnecessarily restrictive, as both Grant Osborne and Craig S. Keener suggest?[20] Is it not the genius of God to speak and act in history? Can biblical narrative not be theologically freighted? Does God not have a story and does his activity not generate stories of his character, will, and ways? In other words, doctrine? If so, then does it not follow that all this is true for the Spirit? What is the way forward?

Scripture at times is merely descriptive. Jesus was crucified in the Roman manner, but there is no norm to be drawn from the story for capital punishment and its methods (e.g., Mark 15:21–25). Scripture may also be prescriptive. The love of God and neighbor are not optional (Matt. 22:34–40). Scripture may be proscriptive. The worship of idols is never morally acceptable (1 John 5:21). Lastly, Scripture may be concessive. For example, take Paul's careful discussion of singleness and marriage in the light of "the present distress" (1 Cor. 7:1–40, especially vv. 6 and 26). Narratives are descriptive, but may contain prescriptive or proscriptive or concessive elements. Moreover, they may include didactic elements as actors in the narrative comment or command. As Paul Barnett and Peter Jensen rightly suggest: "We may indeed gather commands, promises, and doctrine from the words of an apostolic speech addressed to the public whether Christian or general."[21]

Peter's interpretation of the events of Pentecost and at Cornelius's house are an example of how narrative—in this instance, the story of his report to the Jerusalem leadership—may prove doctrinally instructive. From Peter's speech we learn that what happened to him at Pentecost was the promised baptism with the Spirit, and that too was Cornelius's experience. Apart from that comment there is no other text in Acts that explicitly and retrospectively links both

---

[19]Sinclair Ferguson, *The Holy Spirit* (Leicester: Inter-Varsity, 1996), 84 (original emphasis).
[20]For a spirited defense of the appeal to narrative to establish doctrine, see Grant Osborne, *The Hermeneutical Spiral: A Comprehensive Introduction to Biblical Interpretation* (Downers Grove, IL: InterVarsity, 1991), 172; and Craig S. Keener, *Gift Giver: The Holy Spirit for Today* (Grand Rapids, MI: Baker Books, 2002), 209–13.
[21]Paul Barnett and Peter Jensen, *The Quest for Power* (Sydney, Australia: Anzea, 1973), 15. Also see the useful discussion in Gordon D. Fee, *Gospel and Spirit: Issues in New Testament Hermeneutics* (Peabody, MA: Hendrickson, 1991), 83–104, especially his helpful distinctions between "normal," "repeatable," and "normative."

the baptism with the Spirit and the events of Pentecost (cf. Acts 1:5; 2:1–41; 10:44–48; 11:15–18).[22] Likewise, Stephen's speech is full of theological insight into salvation history and how the divine project unfolded over time according to the Law and the Prophets. He masterfully connects the Abraham story, Joseph story, Moses story, and Solomon story in a framework of promise and fulfillment, quoting and alluding to Old Testament Scripture in doing so (e.g., Gen. 12:1; Ex. 2:13–14; 3:6; 32:1; Deut. 18:15; Amos 5:25–27; Isa. 61:1–2). David Peterson comments: "The wisdom given to Stephen clearly informs his interpretation of the Scripture in [Acts] 7:1–53."[23]

External Call and Internal Call

The debates between Calvinists and Arminians over whether the call of God to believe the gospel may be resisted is often discussed in terms of a distinction between an external and an internal call.[24] The external call is the gospel heard with one's outward ears. The internal call is the gospel heard in one's heart and made efficacious by the Holy Spirit. Hence the internal call has also been termed the "effectual" or "effective" call (Grudem and Vanhoozer, respectively).[25] Lydia serves as a case in point. She heard Paul's words, but in addition the Lord opened (*diēnoixen*) her heart to pay attention to them (Acts 16:14). Using this distinction, it could be argued that the biblical record shows that the external call of God may be resisted. Both Old and New Testaments have stories that illustrate such resistance (e.g., Psalm 95 and Israel in the wilderness and Acts 7, respectively). With regard to Stephen's speech, on this view his hearers belonged to a long line of God's people who had rejected the external call of God. But the internal call of God, at least

---

[22]John Stott makes a wise general hermeneutical comment: "What I *am* saying is that what is descriptive is valuable only in so far as it is interpreted by what is didactic. Some of the biblical narratives which describe events are self-interpreting because they include an explanatory comment, whereas others cannot be interpreted in isolation but only by the light of doctrinal or ethical teaching which is given elsewhere," John R. W. Stott, *Baptism and Fullness: The Work of the Holy Spirit Today* (London: Inter-Varsity, 1975), 15 (original emphasis).

[23]Peterson, *Prophecy*, 12.

[24]For a discussion of the distinction from a Reformed perspective, see Wayne Grudem, *Systematic Theology: An Introduction to Biblical Doctrine* (Leicester: Inter-Varsity; Grand Rapids, MI: Zondervan, 1994), 692–95.

[25]Cf. Kevin J. Vanhoozer, *First Theology: God, Scripture and Hermeneutics* (Downers Grove, IL: InterVarsity; Leicester: Apollos, 2002), 96; and Grudem, *Theology*, 693, fn. 3.

on the Calvinist view, is always effective because the Spirit can never be defeated.[26] Bruce Demarest puts it well:

> Scripture indicates that *penultimately* people can and do resist the Spirit's operations (Acts 7:51; 26:14; Heb. 12:25). But *ultimately* human resistance does not prevail, for the Spirit exerts on the souls of chosen sinners an influence of sufficient grace and power to cause the Father's saving purpose to bear fruit.[27]

There is mystery here, since human agency is not nullified by the Holy Spirit's own sovereign agency. Stephen's speech is silent concerning the internal call. Thus the Remonstrants were mistaken in using Acts 7 to make their point about the resistibility of grace. If there is a case for such a notion, then it needs to be based elsewhere in Scripture.

Contrasting Responses to the Proclaimed Word

The resistance to the Holy Spirit in Acts 7 culminated in murder. Stephen's hearers were vexed to an extreme (*dieprionto*). They gnashed (*ebryxon*) their teeth. This was their response to the proclaimed Word of God. And it was not the first time in Acts that the council was so enraged. In Acts 5 we learn of Peter's encounter with the same council. He was brought before it (Acts 5:25–28). The high priest had charged Peter and the others not to preach about Jesus (Acts 5:28, "in this name"). Peter refused to comply. He was under higher orders: "We must obey God rather than men" (Acts 5:29). Peter repeated the charge that the Jewish authorities had killed Jesus (Acts 5:30, note the emphatic use of the personal pronoun "you," plural, *hymeis*). But now Christ is vindicated, raised from the dead, exalted at God's right hand (Acts 5:31). Peter and the others are witnesses to this extraordinary reversal. And, significantly, so too is the Holy Spirit (Acts 5:32). The implication is clear. Rejecting the apostolic testimony is rejecting the Holy Spirit's testimony. The council,

---

[26]Anthony A. Hoekema, *Saved by Grace* (Grand Rapids, MI: Eerdmans, 1989), 86. For an Arminian alternative view, see Leslie D. Wilcox, "Effectual Calling," Richard S. Taylor, ed., *Beacon Dictionary of Theology* (Kansas City, MO: Beacon Hill Press, 1983), 181: "The total teaching of the Bible is that the gospel call is an open call, an unrestricted call, and an enabling call to those who respond favorably."
[27]Demarest, *The Cross*, 84–85 (my emphases).

except for wise Gamaliel, is outraged. The members are angry in the extreme: "When they heard this, they were enraged and wanted to kill them" (Acts 5:33–34). The same Greek word (*diaprio*) is used to describe their reaction as is used later to describe the council's reaction to Stephen. The episode, in fact, anticipates in its own way Stephen's experience in Acts 7.

However, not all who heard the Spirit's testimony reacted with such rage. At Pentecost Peter was as direct with the crowd as he was later to be with the council. He said to the crowd: "Let all the house of Israel therefore know for certain that God has made him both Lord and Christ, this Jesus *whom you crucified*" (Acts 2:36). The listeners took the point: "Brothers, what shall we do?" (Acts 2:37). Peter called for their repentance, and about three thousand were baptized and added to restored Israel (Acts 2:38–41). Significantly, the narrative tells us that "they were cut [*katenygēsan*] to the heart" (Acts 2:37). The force of the Greek suggests real sorrow at the core of one's being.

Even more impressive is the reaction of the Bereans in a later Acts narrative. Paul had traveled to Berea from Thessalonica after a mob riot (Acts 17:1–9). He and Silas preached the gospel in the synagogue (Acts 17:11). And how were they received? The narrative relates, "Now these Jews were more noble than those in Thessalonica; they received the word [*ton logon*, the gospel] with all eagerness, examining the Scriptures daily to see if these things were so" (Acts 17:11). These Bereans welcomed the word. The Greek (*edexanto*) suggests that they enthusiastically embraced this word (Acts 17:11). In this the narrative informs us they were more noble than the Thessalonians (Acts 17:11). This value judgment makes it clear how the Word of God is to be appropriately heard (cf. Acts 8:14; 11:1). However, it must be observed that some of the Thessalonians (e.g., Jason) had become believers (Acts 17:4–5). In fact, Paul writes in his letter to the Thessalonians: "When you received [*paralabontes*] the word of God, which you heard from us, you accepted [*edexasthe*, a different aspect of the same verb found in Acts 17:11] it not as the word of men but as what it really is, the word of God, which is at work in you believers" (1 Thess. 2:13).

Such very different reactions to the Word of God in the Acts narrative should caution us against any mechanical understanding of what elicits a positive response to the message. I recall some years ago being told by an evangelist that in door-to-door evangelism the response rate to a particular little booklet presentation of the gospel was one in four in the United States but one in seven in Australia. This statistic was used as an incentive to encourage us to go out into the hot Australian sun and win people for Christ (at least one in seven). I remember wondering at the time what the need was for the Holy Spirit and prayer since we had statistics on our side. I was disquieted. Today, I would say that his advice was based on a faulty theological anthropology and a flawed hamartiology (doctrine of sin). Outside of Christ we are dead in our sins (Eph. 2:1–10). Without the Spirit's enabling, none would embrace the message.

I wonder if at times at an operational level—not at least at an espoused one, I would hope—an evangelical version of the Socratic fallacy is at work. The Socratic fallacy is the view that to know the truth is to do it. And so if we properly inform people of the truth of the gospel, then they should embrace it. A contemporary refinement of the Socratic fallacy is what might be termed the technocratic fallacy. Another evangelist, this time a British one, shared with me that he had consulted a social psychologist to help make his appeals for people to come forward at his meetings more successful. As a result of the consultation he now employed the technique of having counselors immediately respond to his appeal and thus fill up the space before the platform and to do so even before any enquirer had responded. The psychologist thought that such a void, if left unfilled, would be a disincentive for people to respond to the appeal. If we know what to say and how to say it and how to create the most favorable environment for a positive response, then it will happen. We have truth and technique on our side. Again, this is often more a case of practice than a thought-out theological position at work.

The doctrine of the internal, effectual call is the way Reformed theology explains different reactions to the heard Word as portrayed in the book of Acts. It does so in terms of the sovereign grace of God at work through the Holy Spirit, in some but not all. But is there then no real part for us to play in the drama of God's reclamation of his estranged creation? Is there a role for us to play that does not fall into either the Socratic fallacy or the technocratic one?

Stephen: Boldness and Prayer

By any measure, Stephen was a bold preacher. He spoke uncomfortable truth to religious power. To the council that had played its role in Jesus' death, and in Peter's, and the others' imprisonment, he told of its part in the killing of the Messiah of Israel. This courage is not a matter of possessing a certain temperament or personality type as far as the Acts account is concerned. Stephen was full of the Holy Spirit. The Spirit was the source of his wisdom. But what of his boldness?

The answer to that question lies in an earlier Acts narrative. According to Acts 4, Peter was brought to a gathering of religious authorities ("rulers and elders and scribes") in Jerusalem, which included "Annas the high priest and Caiaphas and John and Alexander, and all who were of the high-priestly family" (Acts 4:5–6). On the previous day, Peter had been discovered in the temple proclaiming the resurrected Christ. He was promptly arrested (Acts 4:1–3). Now filled with the Spirit and before the gathering, Peter preaches boldly: "Let it be known to all of you and to all the people of Israel that by the name of Jesus Christ of Nazareth, whom you [*hymeis*, emphatic] crucified, whom God raised from the dead—by him this man [the story of the healing is in Acts 3:1–9] is standing before you well" (Acts 4:8–13). Because of fear of public reaction, the apostles were released from custody (Acts 4:21).

The next part of the narrative is particularly instructive for our purposes. When the apostles rejoined the rest of the disciples ("their friends") they reported what had just transpired. (Was Stephen there?) The response was a prayer. They called upon the "Sovereign Lord," the Creator and Revealer, whose predestinating purposes had come to pass in the story of Jesus' death (Acts 4:24–28). The burden of their prayer was straightforward: "And now, Lord, look upon their threats and grant to your servants to continue to speak

[*lalein*, present infinitive active] your word with boldness [*parrēsia*]"
(Acts 4:29). The prayer was answered immediately. The place shook
and they were all filled with the Holy Spirit and continued to speak
[*elaloun*, imperfect aspect] the word of God with boldness [*parrēsia*]
(Acts 4:31). And so in the next chapter we find Peter speaking truth
to the religious authorities with such boldness and likewise in the
following two chapters with Stephen (Acts 5:17–42 and 6:8–7:60,
respectively). Luke as both a theologian and an historian has carefully juxtaposed these accounts. Indeed, the book of Acts ends on
the same note, with the apostle Paul "proclaiming the kingdom of
God and teaching about the Lord Jesus Christ with all boldness"
(Acts 28:31; also see the use of the verb *parrēsiazomai* in Acts
9:27–28; 13:46; 14:3; 18:26; 19:8; 26:26).

The Holy Spirit was the source of the boldness of these early
Christians as exemplified in Peter, Stephen, and Paul. But praying
for boldness, rather than for the Holy Spirit's filling per se, was the
part played by the church as the Acts narrative shows. And as our
culture moves from apathy with regard to Christianity to, at times,
contempt or gratuitous dismissal, then boldness is needed all the
more. Moreover, as some of the leadership of some well-known
denominations consciously and intentionally moves away from
biblical moorings in matters of faith and morals, then again boldness is needed all the more. And as militant forms of Islam persecute
Christian believers in various parts of the globe, then again boldness
is needed all the more. I remember a dramatic lunchtime conversa-
tion with two overseas students about to return to their respective
homelands after completing their theological studies. One was
from Pakistan and the other from Northern Nigeria. The Christian
from Pakistan expected to be killed within five years; the Nigerian
thought that he would only be beaten several times in that same
period and maybe have his house burned down more than once.
(Since then the situation in Northern Nigeria has become far more
deadly for Christians.) I merely listened in as they spoke enthusiastically about the opportunities to preach the gospel in their respective
contexts. All those references in the Gospels to carrying one's cross
literally applied to my two friends in ways that I could only imagine,

living as I do in the comfortable West. But such boldness will not be found without calling upon the name of the sovereign Lord, whose gospel it is.

CONCLUSIONS

As we have seen, only once in the New Testament is resisting the Holy Spirit explicitly mentioned (Acts 7:51). It is how Stephen summed up Israel's consistent rejection of the Word of God in promise, law, prophecy, Jesus, and his own testimony. From the Acts narrative it is clear that Stephen's own reading of his Old Testament Scriptures in the light of Christ and his application to the attitudes and actions of his hearers was an expression of a wisdom sourced in the Holy Spirit. Resisting Stephen's testimony was resisting the Holy Spirit. Although, historically speaking, some have seen in the text great relevance to the debate between Calvinists and Arminians, the text has other concerns. In today's world we resist the Holy Spirit by resisting the Word of God, which the Spirit has inspired, its faithful interpretation and application. The boldness to speak such a word especially to those in power, whether in the church or outside it, is a very great need. The apathy and hostility of others so easily mutes the Christian's voice. The early Christians portrayed in Acts faced hostility, not apathy, as far as we can tell. In such a context, they were aware of the very great need to call upon God, in frank recognition of his sovereignty, to grant a boldness that mere temperament cannot generate. They needed a freedom to speak truth to culture as well as power. The need remains.

chapter three

OUGHT WE TO PRAY TO
THE HOLY SPIRIT?

OUGHT WE TO PRAY TO THE SPIRIT? The question is an important one. For the fact is that some Christians as a practice of life have done so in the past and do so in the present. But the use of that word *ought* raises the question to a significantly higher level than simply asking, "Do Christians pray to the Spirit?" *Ought* brings with it the sense of moral obligation.

I want to address the question by first looking at the practice of praying to the Spirit in the past as well as contemporary support for such prayer. Next I will turn to the biblical testimony, since Scripture as the Word of God written provides the quality assurance for our theological ideas and the touchstone for our practices. Lastly, I will offer a theological reflection upon what was presented. Theological reflection, to justify the descriptor "theological," asks the normative questions: "Well, what then ought we to believe about praying to the Spirit?" and "How are we to live out our answer?"

PRAYING TO THE SPIRIT:
SOME PAST AND PRESENT PERSPECTIVES

As Max Turner points out, the earliest example of worship addressed to the Holy Spirit is found in the second-century *Martyrdom and*

Ascension of Isaiah (9:33–36).[1] Within a couple of centuries we find in the Niceno-Constantinopolitan Creed that both the East (Greek speaking) and West (Latin speaking) were confessing that the Spirit, along with the Father and the Son, "is worshipped together and glorified together."[2] However, according to Leonard Hodgson, prayers specifically addressed to the Holy Spirit are hard to find before the tenth century.[3] For example, we do have prayers such as this one from William of St. Thierry, who died in the twelfth century, which begins: "O God, Love, Holy Spirit, Love of the Father and the Son and their substantial will."[4] And there are hymns in the Western church that are invocations addressed to the Holy Spirit, as in Bianco da Sienna's (d. A.D. 1434) great pneumatological hymn, "Come down, O Love divine." The hymn is redolent with biblical allusions.

> *Come down, O Love divine,*
> *Seek Thou this soul of mine,*
> *And visit it with Thine own ardour glowing,*
> *O Comforter, draw near,*
> *Within my heart appear,*
> *And kindle it, Thy Holy flame bestowing.*[5]

Contemporary Anglicanism includes, in more than one of its prayer books, prayers addressed to the Holy Spirit. For example, in *A Prayer Book for Australia* this prayer is found in the Monday morning service: "Creator Spirit, Advocate promised by our Lord Jesus: increase our faith and help us to walk in the light of your presence."[6]

---

[1]Max Turner, "'Trinitarian' Pneumatology in the New Testament—Towards an Explanation of the Worship of Jesus," *The Asbury Theological Journal*, vol. 57/vol. 58, no. 2/no. 1 (Fall 2002/Spring 2003): 168.
[2]Henry Bettenson, ed., *Documents of the Christian Church*, 2nd ed. (London, Oxford, and New York: Oxford University Press, 1967), 26. George S. Hendry argues that "the most glaring—and fateful—defect in this Creed is the absence of any statement concerning the relation of the Holy Spirit to Christ" (*The Holy Spirit in Christian Theology* [Philadelphia: Christian Press, 1956], 38). Bettenson's criticism is puzzling because in the second article of this same creed it states that "Christ was made flesh of the Holy Spirit and the Virgin Mary," Bettenson, ibid.
[3]Leonard Hodgson, *The Doctrine of the Trinity* (Welwyn, UK: James Nisbet, 1972), 232.
[4]Quoted in Bernard McGinn and Patricia Ferris McGinn, *Early Christian Mystics: The Divine Vision of the Spiritual Masters* (New York: Crossroad, 2003), 255.
[5]For the complete text of the hymn, see http://www.hymnsite.com/lyrics/ umh475.sht (accessed May 21, 2006).
[6]*A Prayer Book for Australia: Shorter Edition* (Sydney: Broughton, 1995), 391.

In so doing they are in step with that classic expression of Anglican spirituality, *The Book of Common Prayer* of 1662. In its litany we pray to each person of the Trinity, Father, Son, and Holy Spirit, as well as to the Trinity per se. The Spirit is addressed in the following way: "O God the Holy Ghost, proceeding from the Father and the Son: have mercy upon us miserable sinners."[7]

Present-day Roman Catholicism likewise provides prayers for the faithful that directly address the Holy Spirit. There is, for example, a "Litany of the Holy Spirit" for private use. The Spirit is called upon with a variety of descriptors, including "Ray of heavenly light," "Author of all good," "Consuming fire," "Comforter," and "Sanctifier." The Spirit is petitioned to provide a variety of goods, including to convict of sin, to inflame us with love, and to teach prayer. Lastly, the Spirit is invited: "Come, Holy Spirit! Fill the hearts of Thy Faithful."[8]

Orthodoxy both past and present has had a robust pneumatological tradition in theology and liturgy. Indeed, one of the claims of Orthodoxy is that it represents a more balanced view of the relation between the two hands of God—the Son and the Spirit—than the Western Christians have shown with their lopsided accent on Christology (represented in their championing of the *filioque* addition to the Niceno-Constantinopolitan Creed). In fact, the Orthodox prayer book opens with a prayer to the Holy Spirit. Indeed, every morning the faithful of this church pray as they were taught to do from the time that they were little children: "Heavenly King, Paraclete, Spirit of truth, who art present everywhere and fillest all things, Treasury of goodness and Giver of life, come, dwell in us and cleanse us from all stain, and, of thy mercy, save our souls. Amen."[9]

Invoking the Holy Spirit directly is also a feature of charismatic and Pentecostal piety. For example, in the Anglican church that I

---

[7]*The Book of Common Prayer*, http://www.eskimo.com/~lhowell/bcp1662/daily/litany.html (accessed July 4, 2006).
[8]"Litany of the Holy Spirit," http://www.ewtn.com/devotionals/pentecost/pent13.htm (accessed July 4, 2006).
[9]Quoted in Parthenios, Patriarch of Alexandria and All Africa, "The Holy Spirit," Michael Kinnamon, ed., *Signs of the Spirit: Official Report of the Seventh Assembly* (Geneva: WCC, 1991), 32.

attend there have been occasions when a member of the ministry team has called upon the Holy Spirit to come and to sweep through the congregation with love or power.

Enough then of examples—it is clear that calling upon the Holy Spirit by name in prayer has had a very long history in a variety of Christian traditions. The question, though, is how well grounded, exegetically speaking, is such a practice and if it is not, may it be justified another way? If so, then just how much obligation does that justification bring with it?

PRAYER IN BIBLICAL TESTIMONY

I am using the word *prayer* in a portmanteau way to cover a range of biblical practices which address God. These include adoration, thanksgiving, confessing sin, lament, and petition. To make the discussion more manageable, my focus will largely be on petitionary prayer.

The Importance of Prayer

The importance of prayer in biblical perspective cannot be gainsaid. Luke's Gospel in particular shows that Jesus both prayed as a practice of life and taught his disciples what to pray. Having just prayed himself, Jesus was asked by one of his disciples: "Lord, teach us to pray, as John taught his disciples" (Luke 11:1). Their request is illuminating. John the Baptist is so often thought of in terms of his eccentric dress sense (camel's hair), unusual diet (locusts and wild honey), fiery preaching of repentance and judgment, and the baptizing of Jesus (cf. Matt. 3:1–12; Luke 3:1–21). But as a teacher of prayer? This is an aspect of the Baptizer's ministry that is seldom noted.

In the Lukan narrative flow, Jesus proceeded to teach a version of the famous Lord's Prayer, which consists of petition after petition addressed to the Father and about the kingdom (Luke 11:1–4). Significantly then, discipling others involved teaching followers how to relate to God in prayer, both for John the Baptist and Jesus. Living this side of the invention of the printing press, have we evangelicals lost something of singular importance if we disciple people in Bible reading to the neglect of teaching how the new Christian is to relate to God in prayer? Put another way, do we leave a spirituality vacuum? If we do, I suspect that other sorts of spirituality will fill the void. These practices may be drawn from Orthodoxy, or Roman Catholicism, or the Christian mystical tradition, or even from contemporary therapeutic practices such as imagining Jesus seated opposite you in the quietness of your room. Speak to him as you might speak to, say, an absent sibling whom you deeply miss. I am deeply grateful for the fact that when I was a new Christian, an older Christian took the trouble to teach me how to pray by inviting me to pray with him on a regular basis. I learned by observing him and being taught by him about prayer from the Scriptures. He also taught me to read the Bible regularly and systematically.

The book of Acts narrates an incident in the life of the earliest church that further reinforces the importance of prayer. The apostles are burdened with the problem of pastoral care for Greek-speaking widows who were dependent upon some form of daily distribution. The Hebrew-speaking widows had apparently been prioritized (Acts 6:1). The answer was apostolic delegation (Acts 6:3). But why were they so keen to give the responsibility to others—albeit men of good reputation, Spirit-filled, and wise? Their answer is instructive. The apostles desired to give their attention "to prayer and to the ministry of the word [the gospel]." Apostolic ministry was not reducible to the ministry of the Word. Apostolic ministry was one of Word *and* prayer.

Luke–Acts is not the only biblical witness to the significance of prayer. Paul too is an important contributor to the picture. In 1 Timothy we find the apostle's desires for congregational life at Ephesus. When the household of God meets, it needs sound doctrine and leadership, and Timothy is to ensure that the Scriptures are read publicly and that exhortation takes place (1 Tim. 4:13). But how often have we noticed that the first practice Paul mandates is prayer: "I urge, then, first of all [*prōton pantōn*], that requests, prayers, intercession and thanksgiving be made for everyone—for kings and all those in authority, that we may live peaceful and quiet lives in all godliness and holiness" (1 Tim. 2:1–2 NIV).

Prayer is clearly important, but to whom should it be addressed in particular?

Prayer to the Father

Jesus famously taught disciples in the Sermon on the Mount that prayer is addressed to our Father in heaven: "Pray then like this: 'Our Father in heaven, hallowed be your name'" (Matt. 6:9). This was his own practice, as his so-called high-priestly prayer in the fourth Gospel shows (John 17). In that prayer he prays to his "Holy Father" and "righteous Father" (John 17:11, 25, respectively). The practice of praying to the Father continues in the Pauline epistles (e.g., Eph. 3:14–21; Col. 1:3–14; 1 Thess. 1:2–3) and the Petrine ones (e.g., 1 Pet. 1:3, 17).

But what of praying to Jesus?

Prayer to the Son

There are very few biblical texts that have Jesus himself as the addressee of New Testament prayers compared to prayers addressed to the Father or God. Stephen, that early Christian martyr, provides a well-known example in Acts. As he was being stoned by the enraged mob he called out: "Lord Jesus, receive my spirit" (Acts 7:59). However, there is an earlier example found in the first chapter. The disciples pray to the Lord concerning the selection of a replacement for Judas, and the wider context makes it clear that the ascended Christ is the addressee (cf. Acts 1:6, 21, 24; also see Acts 8:22; 13:2).[10] Paul's first Corinthian letter may suggest a more sustained practice of prayer to Jesus: "All those who in every place call [*epikaloumenois*, participle, present, middle] upon the name of our Lord Jesus Christ" (1 Cor. 1:2), and Paul himself prays to Jesus his Lord as he closes the epistle (1 Cor. 16:22), saying "*Maranatha*" (Aramaic, "O Lord, come!"). Furthermore, Paul prayed to the Lord three times with regard

---

[10]I owe these further examples to Dr. David Peterson, Principal of Oak Hill College.

to the problematic thorn in the flesh that he experienced (2 Cor. 12:8–10). Still further, the letter to the Hebrews argues that Jesus is our great high priest and as such is to be approached with our needs (Heb. 4:14–18). Finally, the canon of Scripture ends with both the bride of Christ (the church) and the Spirit calling upon the Lord to come (Rev. 22:17, 20).

But what of praying to the Spirit?

Prayer to the Spirit

I cannot offer a biblical theology of prayer to the Spirit, as there are no texts that can be used in evidence. Invoking Ezekiel 37:9 is a possible exception, but not on closer inspection.: "Prophesy to the breath; prophesy, son of man, *and say to the breath.*" The result is a vision of dead Israel brought back to life (Ezek. 37:9–14). But the passage is metaphor laden and there is a translation issue as to whether *rûah* is to be rendered "spirit," "Spirit," or "breath." Moreover, even if the Holy Spirit is on view the context is exceptional, namely a prophetic visionary experience. With regard to the New Testament, the Pauline epistles do speak of praying in the Spirit (e.g., Eph. 6:18; also Jude 20) and of the Spirit praying in believers for believers (Rom. 8:26). However, there are no examples of biblical characters praying to the Holy Spirit and there are no commands to pray to the Holy Spirit.

This phenomenon cries out for theological reflection on the part of any serious reader of Scripture.

THEOLOGICAL REFLECTION

The argument for praying to the Holy Spirit, where there are no biblical precedents to call upon, nor explicit texts to cite, is a Trinitarian one. The Trinity is the only God there is: Three persons in one substance. The Father is God, the Son is God, and the Holy Spirit is God. Each person of the triune Godhead is eternally distinct. Prayer to the Holy Spirit is consistent with a robust trinitarianism, one might argue. Let us look, then, at the trinitarian defense of the practice in more detail.

The Trinitarian Defense

In the seventeenth century, John Owen (1616–1683), the magisterial Puritan divine, argued that since God is triune each person of the Godhead is to be communed with by the believer.[11] In the case of the Holy Spirit, he is to be worshiped not because of any role he plays such as that of our comforter, but because he is God.[12] God *qua* God is entitled to our worship. With regard to the Spirit there is the further motivation for praying to the Spirit in that he is the Comforter. Owen maintains that just as Jesus instructed his disciples to believe in God and also in him, so too we are to believe in the Spirit (John 14:1).[13] What is good for Christology is good for pneumatology. Hence the Spirit is to be loved, worshiped, praised, glorified, and prayed to as well as believed.[14] Furthermore, to worship any person of the Trinity is to worship them all.[15]

Last century, Karl Barth was in no doubt about the propriety of praying to the Holy Spirit. In his commentary on the *Apostles' Creed according to Calvin's Catechism* he wrote:

> According to the New Testament, the Holy Spirit is one of the objects of faith. The Creed too declares in conformity with the New Testament: I believe in the Holy Ghost. The Holy Spirit, object of faith, is also an object of prayer: we must not only pray that we may receive the Holy Spirit. *We must pray to him.* "Veni creator spiritus." A Christian's prayer will always be directed to the Holy Spirit also.[16]

Unfortunately, Barth's bold contention, despite its confident appeal to the New Testament, provides no biblical text to back it up.

In our own day, J. I. Packer defends prayer to the Spirit in implicit Trinitarian terms. In his major work on the Spirit, *Keep in Step with the Spirit*, Packer concludes his contribution with two pages on the question of praying to the Holy Spirit. He asks whether it is "proper"

---

[11]William H. Goold, ed., *The Works of John Owen*, vol. 2 (Edinburgh: Banner of Truth Trust, 1980), 9–17.
[12]Ibid., 269–70.
[13]Ibid.
[14]Ibid., 270–71.
[15]Ibid., 268.
[16]Karl Barth, *The Faith of the Church*, trans. Gabriel Vahanian (Cleveland and New York: Meridian, 1963), 130 (my emphasis).

to pray to the Spirit and then acknowledges that there is no biblical example to follow. However, since it is biblically proper to pray to the Father and to the Son, likewise to the Spirit. However, he adds a qualification: "Prayer to the Spirit will equally be proper [as praying to Jesus is] when what we seek from him is closer communion with Jesus and fuller Jesuslikeness [sic.] in our lives."[17]

Both Owen and Packer stand in the Reformed theological tradition. But other Trinitarians argue similarly concerning the propriety of praying to the Spirit. For example, in a sadly neglected little book, Charles W. Lowry discusses the doctrine of the Trinity in relation to Christian devotion. He raises the question of separate prayer to the Father, the Son, and the Spirit. He contends: "If, however, the doctrine of the Trinity is true, there is ample warrant for the address of prayer to the several Persons of the Trinity and to the Trinity itself."[18] In the light of a long tradition in the churches to invoke the Holy Spirit for ordination, he argues "that we ought to go further and in our practice of private meditations, Bible reading, and prayer learn to invoke regularly and confidently God the Holy Spirit."[19] His rationale is that "it is God the Holy Spirit who in His distinct operation and presence is closest to us and most completely within us."[20] Significantly his argument makes scant use of Scripture, apart from a rather obscure use of Paul's temple of the Holy Spirit "metaphor."[21]

For the Trinitarian Christian the argument is hard to withstand. But the scriptural silence is concerning. In the light of that silence the biblical revelation needs revisiting and further reflection is called for.

The Trinitarian Shape of Prayer

If the Old Testament teaches us that there is only one Creator, Revealer, Redeemer God without rival, then the New Testament

---

[17]J. I. Packer, *Keep in Step with the Spirit*, 2nd ed. (Grand Rapids, MI: Baker Books; Leicester: Inter-Varsity, 2005), 207.
[18]Charles W. Lowry, *The Trinity and Christian Devotion* (London: Eyre and Spottiswoode, 1946), 122.
[19]Ibid., 123.
[20]Ibid.
[21]Ibid., fn. 2.

reveals that the single name of God is complex: Father, Son, and Holy Spirit (cf. Deut. 6:4–5; Matt. 28:18–20). Moreover, the canon of Scripture reveals a God on a mission. As Christian novelist Frederick Buechner has said, "The Good Book is a good book."[22] He maintains that despite the diversity of biblical testimonies the essential plot is quite simple: God creates the world, the world gets lost, and God restores the world to its glory.[23] Similarly, theologian Stephen Sykes sees in Scripture the four elements of the "grammar of narrative": the setting, the theme, the plot or plots, and the resolution. On his view:

> In Christian narrative, God's world is the *setting*, the *theme* is the rescue of the fallen world and of humankind; the *plots* are the biblical narratives, from creation, election, to incarnation, crucifixion, resurrection and ascension; the *resolution* is the last judgement, heaven and hell.[24]

Sykes gives more precise material content to Buechner's "The Good Book is a good book." God has a project.

More specifically, the metanarrative of Scripture reveals the divine plan to be nothing less than to have his people, in his place, under his rule, living his way, in his holy and loving presence as family. In fact, the created order longs to see this revelation according to Paul (Rom. 8:18–25). Moreover, the finale will take nothing less than a new heaven and a new earth as its stage (Revelation 21–22). Indeed, the entire renewed world is a worship space no longer in need of any physical temple because of the presence of God and the Lamb (Rev. 22:1–4).

However, there is a shape to the outworking of this plan: *from* the Father *through* the Son *by* the Spirit and *to* the Father *through* the Son *by* the Spirit. Scripture is a comedy in the literary sense—a U-shaped epic that moves from glory through tragedy to glory.[25] The *exitus* (outgoing) and *reditus* (return) are archetypally lived

---

[22]F. Buechner, "The Good Book as a Good Book," in *The Clown in the Belfry: Writings on Faith and Fiction* (San Francisco: HarperSanFrancisco, 1992), 44.

[23]Ibid.

[24]S. Sykes, *The Story of Atonement* (London: Darton, Longman and Todd, 1997), 14 (original emphases).

[25]Leland Ryken, *The Literature of the Bible* (Grand Rapids, MI: Zondervan, 1980), 342.

out by the Christ. Philippians 2:5–11 magnificently presents his journey from glory through tragedy to glory. His story becomes that of his people and his creation (cf. Hebrews 1–2; Genesis 1–2; Revelation 21–22).

As an important dimension of his returning creation to the Father (1 Cor. 15:24–28), Jesus taught his disciples to pray to their heavenly Father and in his name (Matt. 6:9 and John 15:16, respectively). That is to say, to pray in ways that reflect his character, his mission, and passions. Moreover, with respect to the coming of the Paraclete he did not tell his disciples that he would ask the Spirit to come, but rather that he would ask the Father to send the Spirit: "And I will ask the Father, and he will give you another Helper, to be with you forever" (John 14:16).[26] The Spirit is the promise of the Father. Paul bowed the knee to the Father of our Lord Jesus Christ and taught that the Spirit is the one who gives us access to the Father through Christ the peacemaker (Eph. 3:14 and 2:18, respectively).

Christian praying has a Trinitarian shape, but if the Father is so often the addressee, why are there prayers addressed to Jesus as well? And such biblical prayers there are as we have already seen. Recall that Stephen, early Christian martyr, is an example (Acts 7:59). Recall also that Paul's first Corinthian letter may suggest a more sustained practice of prayer to Jesus (1 Cor. 1:2) and that Paul himself prayed to Jesus his Lord with regard to the thorn in the flesh that he experienced (2 Cor. 12:8–10). Recall further that the letter to the Hebrews argues that Jesus is our great high priest and as such is to be approached with our needs (Heb. 4:14–18). Even so, the preponderance of biblical evidence is that prayer is addressed to the Father. Why is this so?

The Evangelical Shape of Prayer

By "evangelical shape" I mean the gospel shape of Christian praying. The reason that the Father is mostly the addressee of Christian prayer and the Son occasionally the addressee of Christian prayer lies in the nature of the gospel itself, and that for two chief reasons.

---

[26]A point well made by Edwin H. Palmer, *The Holy Spirit*, rev. ed. (Philadelphia: Presbyterian and Reformed, 1971), 137.

The first reason lies in Jesus' mediatorial role as our great high priest, and the second in the enormous privilege of our adoption into the family of God. As our great high priest, as mentioned above, Christ represents God to us and us to God. As such Jesus ever lives to intercede for us (Heb. 7:25). He is the one to whom the Old Testament high priesthood pointed. The temporary gives way to the permanent and eternal in him. Prayer in his name assumes his high-priestly office. But more than that, the preeminent blessing of the gospel, as J. I. Packer has so helpfully pointed out, is sonship (*huiothesia*).[27] In fact, although, unlike Paul, not every New Testament witness uses the language of justification, writer after writer, including Paul as we shall see, uses *familial* language of the benefits of the gospel (e.g., John 1:11–12; Heb. 2:10; 1 Pet. 1:13–17; 1 John 3:1–3). By grace we are admitted into the family of God. Moreover, the Spirit of the Son now lives in the believer as the source of his or her new life. Hence the believer prays in Christ (*en tō Christō*), and the prayer language of Jesus (*abba*) becomes his or her own (Rom. 8:15; Gal. 4:6). For the same Spirit that animated his humanity animates our own. And so we pray in Christ's name, not in our own, not in the Spirit's (John 14:16).

A theologian who has carefully considered the scriptural witness on this point is the Scottish theologian James Torrance. According to Torrance:

> The Holy Spirit, through whom we participate in the person and work of Christ, exercises a twofold ministry which in a further way corresponds to the twofold ministry of Christ—namely—of *representing God to humanity* and of *representing humanity to God*.[28]

In his humanity, Christ as our representative is the worshiper par excellence, and our worship through the Spirit is caught up in his own. He concludes: "So in and through the mediatorial ministry of the Spirit, we worship the Father in the name of Christ."[29] More speculatively, Torrance asks whether the wording of Galatians 2:20

---

[27] J. I. Packer, *Concise Theology: A Guide to Historic Christian Beliefs* (Wheaton, IL: Tyndale, 1993), 167.
[28] James B. Torrance, *Worship, Community, and the Triune God of Grace* (Carlisle: Paternoster, 1996), 77 (original emphases).
[29] Ibid.

might be adapted to affirm that when we pray it is not we who pray, but Christ who prays for us, and that our prayers offered in the flesh (our creatureliness) we predicate on the faithfulness of the Christ who loved us and sacrificed himself for us.[30] You may ask: how can this be? His answer is: through Christ and the Spirit. Torrance's contribution has much to commend it. But to speak of the Spirit's mediatorial role when Scripture accents that of Christ is distinctly unhelpful. The economic operations of the triune Godhead need to be carefully distinguished. It is surely no accident that the label used in the earliest church, which has stuck as a descriptor of believers, is "Christian," not "Pneumian."

Coming from a different theological tradition, E. L. Mascall makes a similar case to that of Torrance. He observes how, historically speaking, little liturgical weight has been given to addressing the Spirit. He points out that up until the Arian controversy of the fourth century the doxology of the churches ran "Glory to the Father through the Son in the Holy Spirit." But the Arians, with their view of the ontological inferiority of the Son, appealed to this form of doxology to push their diminished Christology. Hence another form of the doxology became prevalent: "Glory to the Father and to the Son and to the Holy Spirit," or "Glory to the Father with the Son and with the Holy Spirit."[31] From that point on, it was only a short step for some great ones of the Middle Ages, such as Aquinas, to argue that any one of the Godhead could have become incarnate.[32] But according to Mascall:

> The truth is not simply that in Jesus one of the divine Persons has become man, never mind which, but that God-the-Son has become man and that in him manhood has been made filial to the eternal Father. In consequence those who have been adopted into Jesus have been made filial to the Father in Him.[33]

Mascall is on solid biblical ground when he supports this contention by citing Galatians 4:6ff. He concludes: "Thus, *To* the Father,

---

[30]Ibid., 78.
[31]E. L. Mascall, *The Triune God: An Ecumenical Study by E. L. Mascall* (Eugene, OR: Pickwick, 1986 repr.), 37–38.
[32]Ibid., 39.
[33]Ibid., 40.

through the Son, *in* the Spirit becomes not only the pattern of Christian prayer but also the pattern of Christian living."[34]

The Disproportion Question

To pray to the Spirit is not wrong theologically, but if that practice displaces prayer to the Father in the name of the Son in reliance upon the Spirit, then there may be another sort of problem that emerges. The problem is that of disproportion.[35] There are many ways to spoil the gospel. One such way is by addition: Christ plus Mosaic circumcision as the gospel for the Gentiles. Galatians addresses this error. The gospel may also be spoiled by subtraction. Christ is divine but not human. The recently publicized Gnostic *Gospel of Judas* appears to take this road.[36] Jesus is depicted as saying to Judas: "You will be greater than all the others, Judas. You will sacrifice the man that clothes me."[37] This error subtracts human nature from Christ and turns him into only a seeming human. This docetic error was the problem facing the original readers of John's first letter (1 John 4:1–3). But the gospel may also be spoiled by a lack of due weight in theological emphasis, by giving an element in it either too much or too little accent. A biblical truth may be weighted in a way that skews our thinking about God and the gospel. Arguably, to make prayer to the Holy Spirit the principal practice in Christian praying would be such an error. The Holy Spirit may be prayed to. He is God. But the Holy Spirit is not to be prayed to in such a way as to mask the mediatorship of Christ and our location in Christ as members of his body. For to pray to the Father in the name of the Son in reliance upon the Spirit is to rehearse the very structure of the gospel: the sending of the Son by the Father, the sending of the Spirit of the Son from the

---

[34]Ibid. (original emphases).

[35]For a classic discussion of ways in which the gospel may be spoiled, see J. C. Ryle, "Evangelical Religion," in *Knots Untied* (London: Thynne, 1885), 16–17 especially. A further problem in praying to the Spirit may be that since the Spirit lives in the believer, to direct prayer inwards, as it were, may be greatly confusing. As G. K. Chesterton pointed out in *Orthodoxy*, if Jones prays to the God in Jones, Jones may end up praying to Jones; see http:// www.dur.ac.uk/martin.ward/ gkc/books/ortho14.txt (accessed May 22, 2006).

[36]See James M. Robinson, *The Secrets of Judas: The Story of the Misunderstood Disciple and his Lost Gospel* (New York: HarperSanFrancisco, 2006), especially chap. 3, "The Gnostic Judas."

[37]Quoted in "Was Judas Actually a Good Guy?" *Parade*, April 9, 2006, 16.

Father, and our response through the one mediator between God and humankind. In this practice, Christmas, Good Friday, Easter Sunday, and Pentecost are on display.

Observing both the Trinitarian and the evangelical shape of Christian prayer is an important practice to foster or even recover, if unfortunately that is necessary, in our churches. So much praying that I hear amongst evangelicals in the North American context is effectively unitarian: "Dear God please hear, Dear God please bless, Dear God please give," etc. My contention is that by our practices you shall know us. If our espoused theology is Trinitarian but our operational theology is unitarian, whether of God *simpliciter* or Jesus or the Spirit, then eventually our espoused theology catches up. Why should we not think that all religions are the same deep down? After all, do we not all pray, "O God . . . " when in need just as others do? The principle of *lex orandi lex credendi est* ("The law of praying is the law of believing") has never been more relevant, living as we do paradoxically in the context of both postmodern pluralism and militant versions of Islam. Put another way, does our practice of prayer show the uniqueness of Christ as the one mediator between God and humankind?

It was part of the genius of Martin Luther that he realized that Christians in his day needed a reformation in praying. According to William R. Russell:

> For Martin Luther, the reformation was about how the church prays. And in this connection, the primary goal of catechesis was to teach believers to pray. Luther sought to instruct parishioners regarding the one to whom they were to pray, to know what to pray, and to know how to pray. In order to attain this goal, he developed a rather unique educational strategy. Both this goal and the strategy used by Luther to reach it are at the theological core of the Lutheran Reformation. Indeed, a, if not the, distinctive feature of the Lutheran Reformation program is its constant emphasis on reforming the way Christians pray.[38]

Such a reformation may be needed yet again.

---

[38]William R. Russell, "Luther, Prayer, and the Reformation," *Word and World: Theology for Christian Ministry*, vol. 22 no. 1 (Winter 2002): 54.

CONCLUSION

Christians *may* indeed pray to the Spirit. Our God *is* triune. But without biblical precedents and explicit biblical warrants, there is no obligation that the Christian pray to the Spirit. Permission, yes! Obligation, no! If a Christian never prayed to the Spirit in this life, would that be a slighting or a grieving of the Spirit? I think not. But never to pray to God the Father is highly problematical. As charismatic theologian Thomas Smail maintains: "So, it follows from the nature of the gospel and the life of God it reveals, that Christian prayer is properly and characteristically addressed to the Father."[39] We must not allow our systematic theology, working from first principles, to trump our biblical theology, which pays close attention to how God has revealed himself as canonically unfolded. That biblical theology shows that the Spirit's ministry is a floodlight one, as J. I. Packer helpfully suggests.[40] He directs our gaze elsewhere in the adoration of God. In so doing, the practice of prayer to the Father through the Son with the assistance of the Spirit encapsulates the gospel of the one mediator between God and humankind, the man Christ Jesus, who gave himself as a ransom for us all and who poured out the Holy Spirit on that singular Pentecost so that we might be caught up in the Son's own communion—as our Lord, Savior, and elder brother in the household of God—with the Father.

---

[39]Thomas A. Smail, *The Forgotten Father: Rediscovering the Heart of the Christian Gospel* (London: Hodder and Stoughton, 1987), 185.
[40]Packer, *In Step*, 57.

chapter four

HOW DO WE QUENCH
THE HOLY SPIRIT?

EVERY EASTER WE LOOK BACK to what Christ, the bearer of the Spirit, achieved in his dying in our place and how he was vindicated by his being raised from the dead. Pentecost soon follows. On that occasion we look back to how the bearer of the Spirit became the bestower of the Spirit and restorer of Israel. Restored Israel in the person of Paul became the light to the nations that Isaiah spoke of, and one of the communities formed in the wake of the Pauline mission was that of the Thessalonians (cf. Isa. 49:6; Acts 13:47; 17:1–9). In what is most probably the earliest New Testament document, written around A.D. 51, the apostle Paul commands the Thessalonians not to quench the Spirit (1 Thess. 5:19–22). In fact, New Testament scholar Luke Timothy Johnson suggests: "The Thessalonian correspondence marks the probable beginning of Christian literature."[1]

Surprisingly, this Pauline command not to quench the Spirit has had comparatively little sustained theological examination. However, I believe that understanding this command and observ-

---

[1] Luke Timothy Johnson, *The Writings of the New Testament: An Interpretation*, rev. ed. (Minneapolis: Fortress, 1999), 281.

ing it in congregational life is of great contemporary importance. The answer to our question, "How do we quench the Holy Spirit?" will affect our practices. First, we briefly look at what was said in the past about quenching the Spirit—especially by John Calvin and John Owen—and then at what is being said in the present. Next we examine the biblical testimony, and that testimony will also raise the vexing question as to the nature of New Testament prophecy. Finally, I offer a theological reflection on what we have considered before drawing the discussion to a close.

QUENCHING THE SPIRIT:
SOME PAST AND PRESENT PERSPECTIVES

In the sixteenth century Calvin dealt with our question in his commentary on 1 Thessalonians. His discussion is a sustained one and is worth examination. He argues that quenching the Spirit is "when we make void his grace."[2] That quenching of the Spirit does include despising prophecies but goes beyond it: "Yet those also *quench the Spirit* who, instead of stirring up, as they ought, more and more, by daily progress, the sparks that God has kindled in them, do, by their negligence, make void the gifts of God."[3] For Calvin, the Spirit is the Spirit of light and to reject any form of the Spirit's enlightenment is to quench the Spirit.

As for prophecy, Calvin contends:

> [F]or as the Spirit of God illuminates us chiefly by doctrine, those who give not teaching its proper place, do, so far as in them lies, *quench the Spirit,* for we must always consider in what manner or by what means God designs to communicate himself to us. Let every one, therefore, who is desirous to make progress under the direction of the Holy Spirit, allow himself to be taught by the ministry of prophets.[4]

Prophecy, according to Calvin's commentary, is not foretelling the future God intends, but preaching. More specifically, prophecy is

---

[2]John Calvin, *CJCC*, comment on 1 Thess. 5:19.
[3]Ibid., comment on 1 Thess. 5:20.
[4]Ibid. (original emphasis).

"the science of interpreting Scripture, so that a *prophet* is an interpreter of the will of God."[5]

In the century after Calvin's, John Owen, in his magisterial treatment of the Christian's communion with God, deals specifically with what he entitles "The general ways of the saints' acting in communion with the Holy Ghost."[6] Part of his discussion addresses the question of quenching the Spirit as in the 1 Thessalonians 5:19 text. He acknowledges that there were several understandings of the text current in his day. In his view, however, Paul has in mind not the Person of the Holy Spirit, but "his *motions, actings, and operations.*"[7] He uses the analogy of wet wood thrown into a fire. That is what quenching the Spirit is like. The Spirit's aim is to act in ways that promote our growth in grace. But we may hinder his work. As Owen puts it: "'Take heed,' saith the apostle, 'lest, by the power of your lusts and temptations, you attend not to his workings, but hinder him in his good-will towards you; that is, what in you lieth.'"[8] The discussion is general and frustratingly does not deal with the specifics of the text, unlike Calvin's.

Bringing the discussion up to more recent times, in the second half of the twentieth century, D. M. Lloyd-Jones distinguished between grieving the Spirit, which refers to the Christian's individual lack of obedience, and quenching the Spirit, which has to do with Christian corporate life. He understood the Thessalonians' text to refer to resisting the Spirit's "general movement upon your spirit" in a congregational setting.[9] Back in Thessalonica when the Spirit "came upon people" and they began to prophesy, the temptation was to not respond to the prophesying or to discourage those prophesying.[10] This, Lloyd-Jones argues, is quenching the Spirit.

A contemporary theologian, Wayne Grudem, sees in 1 Thessalonians 5:19–21 evidence for his thesis that New Testament proph-

---

[5]Ibid. (original emphasis).
[6]William H. Goold, ed., *The Works of John Owen*, vol. 2 (Edinburgh: Banner of Truth Trust, 1980), 264.
[7]Ibid., 266 (original emphases).
[8]Ibid., 267.
[9]D. M. Lloyd-Jones, *Joy Unspeakable: The Baptism with the Holy Spirit* (Eastbourne: Kingsway, 1985), 206.
[10]Ibid.

ecy stands on a lower level than Old Testament prophecy as far as its authority is concerned. The Thessalonians were to weigh the prophecy they heard and to hold fast to what was good. According to Grudem: "This could never have been said of the words of an OT prophet, or of the authoritative teachings of a NT apostle."[11] True, New Testament prophecy is Spirit impelled, but still it is a lesser form of communication, which is to be open to scrutiny.

Even this brief survey reveals the questions to be addressed. Is quenching the Spirit related to prophecy only, or is there a wider problem in mind of which despising prophecy is one way in which the Spirit is quenched? And what does quenching look like? Is it really like throwing wet wood in a fire? Further, what exactly is the prophesying on view? Is it preaching and Scripture interpretation as Calvin suggests?

THE BIBLICAL TESTIMONY

As we consider the biblical testimony, immediately we are faced with a translation matter. The Christian public is served by many fine translations: ESV, NIV, and NRSV to name a few. The choice is not so much between poor and really good translations. Rather it is between good translations with differing strengths and weaknesses. The ESV, NIV, and NRSV break up 1 Thessalonians 5:19–22 into more than one sentence. The ESV presents three sentences and separates verse 19, which speaks of the Spirit, and verses 20–21, which speak of prophecies. The NIV links the Spirit and prophecies by translating verses 19–20 as one sentence. But then this translation breaks up verses 21–22 into three sentences. The NRSV provides two sentences and separates verse 19 from the rest. However, both the Greek texts that I used in preparation render verses 19–22 as one complex Greek sentence in order to show that here is a unit of thought that connects quenching the Spirit and despising prophecy. So I take it that Paul's concern is not with quenching the Spirit's ministry in general, whether through various members of the congregation or through various spiritual gifts per se, but specifically with prophesying. Of course, as we explore the link

---

[11]Wayne Grudem, "Prophecy, Prophets," in ed. T. D. Alexander and Brian S. Rosner, *NDBT*, 708.

between quenching the Spirit and despising prophecy, a more general principle may emerge. But first things first.[12]

The Rationale Question

As Gordon Fee points out, our text (1 Thess. 5:19–22) surprises the reader, as nothing else in the letter has prepared the way for it.[13] So finding the apostolic rationale for the injunctions about the Spirit, prophecy, and discernment is not easy. Is Paul addressing a misuse of such a charismatic gift at Thessalonica, or is his aim preventative? Literally Paul is commanding them—the imperative is second person plural—not to keep on quenching the Spirit. The verb "to quench" is in the present aspect. But does it have that force here? Scholars are divided.[14] We may not be able to answer these questions definitively. What is clear, however, is that prophecy was a *bona fide* practice in congregational life and one that was sourced in the Holy Spirit, but even so discernment was necessary. Paul's second letter to the Thessalonians shows the necessity for such discernment as he instructs the Thessalonians not to be shaken by purported spirit or word or letter from Paul, if such communication were characterized by an over-realized eschatology as though the day of Christ had already come (2 Thess. 2:1–2).

The Quenching Question

The idea of quenching *(sbennymi)* the Spirit in the Thessalonians' context involves a metaphorical use of lan-

---

[12]Commentators divide on the question of the general versus the particular. For example, Robert L. Thomas argues with reference to quenching the Spirit, "In particular, this is his impartation of specialized capabilities for ministry to others in the body of Christ." "1 Thessalonians," ed. Frank E. Gaebelein, *EBC*, comment on 1 Thess. 5:19–22. However, F. F. Bruce treats 1 Thessalonians as a coherent unit of thought with quenching the Spirit as referring specifically to prophecy, "I Thessalonians,"ed. Bruce M. Metzger, David A. Hubbard and Glenn W. Barker, *WBC*, comment on 1 Thess. 5:19–21. Bruce's position is to be preferred.

[13]Gordon Fee, *God's Empowering Presence: The Holy Spirit in the Letters of Paul* (Peabody, MA: Hendrickson, 2005), 56.

[14]For example, Robert L. Thomas argues with reference to quenching the Spirit that "when Paul commands, 'Stop putting out the Spirit's fire,' as v. 19 might literally be translated, he advocates the cessation of something already being practiced." "1 Thessalonians," comment on 1 Thess. 5:19. However, F. F. Bruce maintains: "It is doubtful if we should press the use of the present imperative with με here and in v. 20 to mean that the recipients are being told to stop doing something they have already begun to do. Like the positive imperatives in vv. 16–18 and 21–22, the negative imperatives in vv. 19 and 20 indicate what they must habitually do (or refrain from doing)." "1 Thessalonians," comment on 1 Thess. 5:19.

guage.[15] The NIV brings this out in a virtual paraphrase of
1 Thessalonians 5:19: "Do not put out the Spirit's fire." In contrast a literal use is found in Ephesians 6:16 in Paul's discussion
of the armor of God. The shield of faith is able to quench the
fiery darts of the wicked one. How this is so is not immediately
obvious, until we learn something of how a Roman shield could
be used to protect the body. If the enemy were employing flam-
ing darts, then the wooden shield (*thyreos* in Greek and *scutum*
in Latin) could be soaked in water to extinguish the darts, which
had been dipped in pitch and then set alight. Returning to the
Thessalonians' context, quenching the Spirit involved a nullify-
ing of the Spirit's work in the congregation.

How this can be so Paul does not tell us. I for one would love
to know how God the Holy Spirit can be quenched—albeit metaphorically speaking. How does one give a theological, let alone
metaphysical, account of that? Perhaps that is asking questions of
little interest to the great apostle. He may simply be speaking not
only metaphorically, but also phenomenologically. That is to say,
he is speaking in terms of appearances, which would fit in with the
non-postulational character of Scripture. Scripture does not theorize
about the essences of things.[16]

Quenching Prophecy

The specific activity on view with regard to quenching the Spirit
is prophecy. But just what was it? Does it refer to Spirit-inspired
applications of the gospel that Paul had preached to the situations of
the hearers? Or were they Spirit-inspired applications of Paul's letter as it was being read out in the congregation?[17] Indeed, Paul put
the entire church under obligation to have his letter read (1 Thess.
5:27). Or were they spontaneous revelations given by the Spirit

---

[15]The verb *sbennymi* is used of quenching fire or things on fire (e.g., Matt. 12:20; 25:3; Mark
9:44, 46, 48; Eph. 6:16; Heb. 11:34; as well as 1 Thess. 5:19). See G. Abbott-Smith, *A Manual
Greek Lexicon of the New Testament*, 3rd ed. (Edinburgh: T. and T. Clark, 1968), 403.
[16]For an ancient example of postulational writing, see Plato's *Timaeus*.
[17]There is some evidence in Acts that prophets could so use letters. For example, take Judas and
Silas as prophets and the letter of the Jerusalem council (Acts 15:22–32, especially vv. 30–32). I
owe this insight to Dr. David Peterson. See his discussion, *Prophecy and Preaching: Acts and the
Church Today* (Buxton, Derbyshire: Fellowship of Word and Spirit, 1997), 5.

through different congregational members concerning the state of the hearers, as 1 Corinthians 14 might suggest?

It seems to me that the letter itself may give some clues as to what prophecy was not. So let us employ the *via negativa* as our method and see what possibilities it leaves. In the first chapter Paul writes of the "gospel" that the Thessalonians had received (1 Thess. 1:5). In the next chapter he calls this gospel "the word of God" that contrasts with a merely human word (1 Thess. 2:13). He does not write of the "prophecy" that they had embraced. Later, he relays information he had received from the risen Christ concerning his return and the state of those Christians who die in the meantime. He describes it as "the word of the Lord" (1 Thess. 4:15). Again, he does not use the language of prophecy to describe it, even though interestingly the communication has an orientation to the future.[18]

The prophecy of which Paul writes then does seem to stand on a lower level than either the gospel Paul preached or the word of the Lord that he shared with the Thessalonians. Grudem appears to be largely right to suggest that this sort of New Testament prophecy does not have the intrinsic authority of Old Testament prophecy.[19] This kind of Thessalonian prophecy needs testing. The word Paul used for "testing" (*dokimazein*) could be used of a variety of critical examinations ranging from scrutinizing people through to testing metals.[20] The need was to sift the genuine from the false. Quality control was essential. The good needs to be sifted from the bad and that good embraced. Evil of every sort was to be avoided.[21]

Let me suggest that whatever else New Testament prophecy

---

[18]It has been suggested that 1 Thess. 5:19–22 has 1 Thess. 4:13–18 in view. But this is unlikely, because in 1 Thess. 5:20 prophecies is plural (*prophēteias*).

[19]See D. A. Carson, *Showing the Spirit: A Theological Exposition of 1 Corinthians 12–14* (Grand Rapids, MI: Baker Books, 2003), 93–100, for a carefully qualified acceptance of Grudem's argument.

[20]The verb *dokimazō* is used primarily of testing, proving, trying metals (e.g., Prov. 8:10; 17:3 LXX), of other things (e.g., Luke 12:56), and of men and women (e.g., 1 Tim. 3:10). See Abbott-Smith, *Manual*, 120.

[21]Robert L. Thomas suggests: "*Ponerou* ('of evil') likewise presents two options: if it is taken as an adjective qualifying *eidous*, the phrase is 'evil kind,' or taken as a substantive, a practical equivalent of the noun *ponerias*, the phrase is 'kind of evil.'" Though the anarthrous adjective in Paul is more frequently adjectival in force, the nature of the present contrast with *to kalon* (v. 21) resolves this particular issue in favor of the substantival use adopted by NIV." "1 Thessalonians," comment on 1 Thess. 5:22.

may have been, it was an oral communication sourced in the Spirit. In Acts it could be a very public phenomenon. At Pentecost, for example, its content was forthtelling the mighty works of God in the gospel (Acts 2:11, *ta megaleia tou theou*; the ESV and NRSV are better than the NIV here, which has "wonders"), and at Corinth, prophetic activity could disclose the secrets of the heart (1 Cor. 14:25).[22] Interestingly, knowing or exposing the moral state of the human heart seemed to be a necessary condition for identifying a prophet for some in the first century, according to Luke 7:36–50 and John 4:1–38. In the former case, Simon the Pharisee thought to himself that if Jesus were a prophet he would know the moral state of the woman showing him such deference by washing his feet with her tears, wiping them with her hair, kissing them and anointing them (Luke 7:39). And in the latter case the woman of Samaria, when confronted with Jesus' knowledge of her marital and extramarital history, declared him to be a prophet (John 4:19). Peter's prophetic discourse on the day of Pentecost confronted the hearers with "this Jesus . . . you crucified and killed by the hands of lawless men" (Acts 2:23).[23] The hearers "were cut [*katenygēsan*] to the heart" (Acts 2:37). Returning to the Thessalonians, as we have already seen, Paul instructed the Thessalonian believers not to despise prophesying and yet called for discernment on their part (1 Thess. 5:19–21). He instructed those at Corinth similarly (1 Cor. 14:29).

In my view there is an argument then that even regular preaching might become prophetic when used of the Spirit to so expose the hearts of the hearers.[24] Such an exposure may be a sufficient condition for recognizing prophetic activity, but not a necessary one. In the book of Acts, Agabus, as prophet and on the basis of the Spirit's revelation to him, was able to predict "a great famine over

---

[22]Like Old Testament prophecy, New Testament prophecy exhibits both forthtelling of God's word and foretelling the future. Carson, *Showing*, 92, especially fn. 56.

[23]See Peterson, *Prophecy*, 7: "The sequence of events in Acts 2 suggests that Peter is acting as prophet when he proclaims the gospel so powerfully."

[24]My view is consistent with that of Anthony C. Thiselton, *The First Epistle to the Corinthians, New International Greek Testament Commentary* (Grand Rapids, MI: Eerdmans, 2000), 1094, and indeed with Calvin's view, John Calvin, trans. John W. Fraser, *The First Epistle of Paul to the Corinthians* (Grand Rapids, MI: Eerdmans, 1960), 271. Also see Peterson: *Prophecy*, p. 13: "Without confusing preaching and prophecy in the strict sense, it is clear from Acts that there can be *a prophetic dimension to authoritative and effective Christian preaching*" (original emphasis).

all the world" (Acts 11:27–28). There is no suggestion in the text that there was any exposure of the moral situation of the hearers on that same occasion.

THEOLOGICAL REFLECTION

What then, theologically speaking, are we to make of Paul's command to the Thessalonians? What are we to believe and practice in today's world in the light of it? Let us explore the need to be open but discerning with regard to the Holy Spirit, and what such discernment in relation to the Spirit might look like.

Open but Discerning

In my view one's eschatology is crucial with regard to the question of the charismata, including the gift of prophecy, and their validity today. Something of the world to come has broken into the Christian's life (Heb. 6:5). But the best is yet to be and that best lies beyond this "present evil age," to use Paul's idiom (Gal. 1:4). Those who hold such an inaugurated eschatology as I do cannot foreclose on what a sovereign and gracious God might do to gift the present-day church. The cessationist argument that canon closure is on view in 1 Corinthians 13:10 ("when the perfect comes") and that the Pastorals (1 Timothy, 2 Timothy, and Titus) show the eclipse of the charismata by the absence of reference to them do not persuade me. With regard to the former argument, the reference in 1 Corinthians 13:10 appears more likely to be a reference to the return of Christ, and additionally 1 Corinthians 1:4–8 places the Corinthians and the exercise of their gifts in the framework of life between the cross and the second coming of Christ and not that of the cross and canon closure. With regard to the Pastorals, the absence of evidence is not necessarily the evidence of absence.

On the other hand, those who are enthusiastic about charismata for today's church seem all too ready to define New Testament terms for gifts too precisely and identify present-day phenomena with New Testament realities too facilely. As John Owen "contends," according to J. I. Packer, imaginatively putting words in Owen's mouth:

> Since one can never conclusively prove that any charismatic mani-
> festation is identical with what is claimed as its New Testament
> counterpart, one can never in any particular case have more than a
> tentative and provisional opinion, open to constant reconsideration
> as time and life go on.[25]

There is then the need for discernment. Certainly Scripture gives every reason for thinking that false teaching and false prophecy will continue to plague the church (Matt. 24:24; 2 Pet. 2:1; 1 John 4:1). And so Christian gullibility—a long-standing problem in Christian history—must be avoided.[26]

Being open to the Spirit but discerning about claims concerning the Spirit is the way forward. I saw a wonderful example of this approach in my days as a theological student. It was chapel night and unexpectedly one of the students strode to the lectern to speak. He declared: "I have come from Jerusalem with a message from God." It seemed to me to that he became rapidly incoherent and wild-eyed. But the principal stayed seated. After what seemed an age, Dr. Knox quietly got up, moved to the lectern, and gently led the student out. The student had had a breakdown of some sort and needed psychiatric care. Some of us asked him why he had not acted sooner. He replied that the man might have been a prophet from God, so he waited to be sure. Discerning what is a genuine work of God's Spirit in today's world is the tricky matter to which we now turn.[27]

Discerning the Spirit

Claims concerning the Spirit need sifting, as we have seen in discussing 1 Thessalonians 5:19–22. Other New Testament writers were aware of the same pastoral need. Like Paul, the apostle John, for

---

[25]This is Packer's imaginative reconstruction of what Owen might have said if confronted with the claims of charismata operating today. J. I. Packer, *A Quest for Holiness: The Puritan Vision of the Christian Life* (Wheaton, IL: Crossway Books, 1990), 221.

[26]See Lucian's comments on Peregrinus for a second-century instance in ed. J. Stevenson, *A New Eusebius* (London: SPCK, 1970), 134–36.

[27]For this section I am drawing upon my article "Religious Experience and Discernment Today," *Reformed Theological Review*, vol. 56 (January–April 1997), no. 1, 10–12. Also see the discussions in A. M. Stibbs and J. I. Packer, *The Spirit within You: The Church's Neglected Possession* (London: Hodder and Stoughton, 1967), 21–25; Craig S. Keener, *3 Crucial Questions about the Holy Spirit* (Grand Rapids, MI: Baker Books, 1996), chap. 3; and A. W. Tozer, *How to Try the Spirits: Seven Ways to Discern the Source of Religious Experiences* (Camp Hill, PA: Christian Publications, 1997).

example, was aware that many spirits are at large in the world. Not all are benign. These spirits need to be tested (*dokimazein*) to see if they are truly from God. According to John, any such spirit that denied the incarnation was actually the anti-Christ at work (1 John 4:1–3). Gullibility is not a Christian virtue, and deception, either self-deception or devilish, is a real possibility.[28] So what criteria then may be brought to bear on this question of discernment?

In Paul's case, his command to those Thessalonians was to stand fast and hold to the traditions (our gospel) that he had taught them by word and letter (1 Thess. 2:13–15). Given the closure of the canon, the first criterion for us, however, is the scriptural test. It is in the Scriptures that we find the apostolic tradition. Therefore we may ask: does that which is claimed have a prima facie analogy with some phenomenon found in the pages of Scripture? For example, a claim to have carried out an exorcism in the name of Jesus and by the Spirit of God has a real possibility of being genuine. Even so, discernment is still required (Matt. 7:21–23).[29] In other words, such a claim is not to be dismissed a priori. Again, a claim along the lines that someone came to a real Christian faith after becoming convinced of his sinfulness, and therefore his need of Christ, through reading a current Christian book is consistent with what we know of the Spirit's work from our New Testament, even though C. S. Lewis's *Mere Christianity* is not mentioned in Scripture, and yet that was the book that had been read.

A second criterion is Christological. Any claimed experience of the Spirit that detracts from the dignity of Christ as truly God and truly human, and from the integrity of his saving work, is not of the Spirit (1 John 4:1–3). We might ask of such a claim questions such as: what place has Christ (both his person and his work) in the alleged experience of the Spirit and in the rhetoric used to explain it? Does the experience preach Christ (as Luther might say)?[30] When Paul thought that the value of Christ's work was being undermined

---

[28]See the stimulating discussion of deception and lying spirits in Michael Welker, *God the Spirit*, trans. John F. Hoffmeyer, (Minneapolis: Fortress, 1994), 84–98.

[29]Clearly the mere parroting that "Jesus is Lord" is no necessary indication that the Spirit of God is at work (cf. 1 Cor. 12:1–3; Matt. 7:21–23).

[30]See Luther's "Preface to the Epistles of St. James and St. Jude," in ed. J. Dillenberger, *Martin Luther: Selections from His Writings* (Garden City, NY: Anchor, 1961), 36.

by the false teachers troubling the Galatians, he said, "Let them be accursed" (Gal. 1:6–10). However, when others preached the right gospel content-wise about Christ at Philippi—albeit for the wrong reasons, namely, to make life in prison for him even harder—he rejoiced (Phil. 1:15–18). Christology was at the heart of Paul's quality assurance. So also with us, especially if the Holy Spirit is invoked. After all, the Spirit is the Spirit of Jesus (Phil. 1:19). He has not come to thematize himself, but Christ (John 14–16). Christology is at the center, not pneumatology.

As I argued in the previous chapter—following that great Christian leader, Bishop J. C. Ryle, of an earlier century—the gospel may be spoiled in a number of ways.[31] We can spoil the gospel by substituting for Christ's saving work on the cross (for example, our good deeds, as Pelagius did). We can spoil Christ's work by adding to it (for example, faith plus circumcision, as in the Galatian error). We can also spoil the gospel by disproportion when secondary biblical accents become primary (for example, clerical clothing). This latter problem of disproportion is particularly relevant to the present discussion. We can spoil the gospel when the New Testament sense of proportion is lost and pneumatology becomes our primary emphasis rather than Christology. The idea in some charismatic circles in the United States, for example, that "the major compass point for moving ahead in active ministry" is not "the cross" any longer but "charisma" is extremely troubling.[32]

The last important test for our purpose is the moral one.[33] The New Testament presents not only an evangel, but also an ethic. So when Paul preached to the Thessalonians and then moved on, he left behind the Word of God (the gospel as in 1 Thess. 1:2–10 and 2:13) and instruction in how these new Christians were to live and please God (an ethic as in 1 Thess. 4:1–8). Moreover, the gift of the *Holy* Spirit means a sanctified life (1 Thess. 4:7–8 especially). Christians are expected to be a community characterized by moral integrity.

---

[31]See his classic essay, "Evangelical Religion," in *Knots Untied* (London: Thynne, 1885), 16–17 especially. The examples are my own, though, not his.

[32]See C. Peter Wagner, *7 Principles I Learned After Seminary* (Ventura, CA: Regal, 2005), 19–20. How this squares with Paul's ministry to the Corinthians of preaching Christ crucified is not at all clear (1 Cor. 2:1–5).

[33]This test is particularly important to Welker, *Spirit*, 85, who draws out its communal application.

This is not only a Pauline concern. One of the problems with which John deals in his first letter concerns a schismatic community, which had set itself up over against that of John's readers (1 John 2:18–19). The schismatics were claiming to love God, but in fact were exhibiting hatred towards John's readers. How can disciples claim to love God whom they cannot see, when so evidently despising the brothers and sisters in Christ whom they can see (1 John 4:7–21)? John drew attention to the anomaly.

Interestingly, the challenge of discerning the Spirit at work continued beyond the New Testament period. Unlike us, the second-century writer of the *Didache* did not have the gift of a closed canon and the printing press to make it readily available. By mid-century it seems that there were a number of traveling Christian "prophets." They were to be welcomed, but also tested. The tests were simple. For example, "If any prophet, speaking in a trance, says, 'Give money (or anything else),' do not listen to him. On the other hand, if he bids you to give it to someone else who is in need, nobody should criticize him."[34] Again, if the prophet's espoused theology and operational theology were in contradiction—that is to say, if he spoke one way and lived another—he is an impostor. Further, if the prophet stays more than two days he is not the genuine article, but a freeloader on other people's faith. Clearly the need for discernment on the part of God's people was ongoing.

All sorts of claims are made these days about the Spirit's present activities. Some even claim that the Spirit has spoken to them, or that a vital part of a Christian's devotional life is allowing the Spirit to speak in the quietness of one's room. There are books that discuss what the Spirit is saying to the churches and which encourage the reader to hear him.[35] Recently, I watched two televangelists discussing how the Holy Spirit told one of them that the Passover

---

[34]Maxwell Staniforth, ed. and trans., *Early Christian Writings* (Harmondsworth: Penguin, 1968), 233. Staniforth translated "prophet" as "charismatist." I have reverted to "prophet." See his footnote 7, 236.

[35]For example, Henry Blackaby, *What the Spirit Is Saying to the Churches* (Sisters, OR: Multnomah, 2003). There is much that is edifying in this book. There is a healthy accent on searching the Scriptures. But readers are invited to "Hear Him Afresh" 53. However, what that would mean in practical terms is not made clear. Expectations are raised. Yet the reader is left with generalities. The same question may be asked of Keener, *Crucial Questions*, 151–53, where he writes of "Hearing God's Voice: A Personal Account." However, his more recent *Gift Giver: The Holy Spirit for Today* (Grand Rapids, MI: Baker Academic, 2002) is more restrained.

offering to that television ministry was to be extended by thirty days so that viewers might receive a blessing if they gave money. And, after all, did the Spirit not speak to Philip and command him to go to the chariot of the Ethiopian eunuch (Acts 8:29), and did the Spirit not tell those at Antioch to set Saul and Barnabas apart for ministry (Acts 13:2)? However, so little is described of what such speaking was like in those scriptural contexts that it is extremely hazardous to generalize from such incidents or from texts addressed to first-century churches.[36]

I suspect that those who relate how the Spirit has spoken to them today are talking about certain strong impressions they have to do X or Y, or to say X or Y, and *that* is the Spirit's speaking to them today. As a new Christian I attended a church that had no formal order of service. We were to be led by the Spirit. Members contributed as the Holy Spirit directed them to do so. But how was I to know when the Spirit wanted me to give a word of encouragement or to contribute a Scripture reading or offer a prayer? I asked one of the older members for advice. His answer was simple: "When your heart gives a bump, then jump." However, I was never able to distinguish between the Spirit and an adrenalin surge.

Sometimes the rhetoric evangelicals, charismatics, and Pentecostals use to articulate Christian experience, whether of the Spirit or Christ, is fundamentally misleading because it is left unnuanced and unexplained.[37] For example, we simplistically explain that relating to the Lord is just like relating to a best friend or a spouse. Your best friend speaks to you and you speak to him or her. But actually, theologically speaking, the Lord has ascended to the right hand of the Father (Acts 1:6–11). We await his return like those Thessalonians did (1 Thess. 1:9–10). Relating to the Lord— just as we relate to our best friend or spouse—is an eschatological prospect. It is our hope (1 John 3:1–2). At present we walk by faith, not by sight (2 Cor. 5:7).[38] Furthermore, philosophically speaking,

---

[36]A point well made by Peter Jensen, "The Spirit of Revelation," in B. G. Webb, ed., *Explorations 6: Spirit of the Living God, Part Two* (Homebush West, NSW: Lancer, 1992), 16–17.
[37]See my "Experiencing the Lord: Rhetoric and Reality," in B. G. Webb, ed., *Spirit of the Living God*, 49–70. In this piece I address the problem arising from the rhetoric that suggests that speaking to God and God speaking to us is just like relating to one's best friend or spouse.
[38]The great contrast in the New Testament is not between faith and reason, but between faith and

we meet our spouse and best friend in an embodied form. In fact, reading their body language is a vital part of the relationship. But in this age we do not meet Jesus in an embodied form. If that is true of relating to the Lord Jesus, how much more so of the Spirit who points away from himself to the truth about Christ?

CONCLUSIONS

As believers in Christ, we do need to be open-minded about the Spirit. Christ has not left us abandoned. We do live this side of Pentecost. The Spirit has indeed come. We are not to quench the Spirit in our congregational life. We should be open to God's using Christian speech to expose our hearts. To quench the Spirit today is to ignore the preached or read Word of God that stirs our consciences, or to oppose ministries that reveal our moral misalignment with the revealed will of God. Although I wonder how that might happen if the gospel is not preached, nor Scripture expounded or read, nor opportunity given in our meetings for the truth of God to be applied to our lives—albeit in less formal ways than the pulpit suggests.[39] Yet we must not be empty-headed. Our consciences may be bound by other than the Holy Spirit and with it our lives spoiled. Discernment was needed in Paul's day and it is still needed today.

---

sight (2 Cor. 5:7) and faith and fear (Mark 4:40).
[39]See David Peterson, *Engaging with God: A Biblical Theology of Worship* (Leicester: Apollos, 1992), 197.

chapter five

HOW DO WE GRIEVE
THE HOLY SPIRIT?

THUS FAR WE HAVE considered blasphemy against the Spirit, resisting the Spirit, whether we ought to pray to the Spirit, and what it means to quench the Spirit. Next we focus on another of Paul's commands addressed to an early Christian congregation, or maybe to more than one of them.[1] The question of Pauline authorship of the letter to the Ephesians is not an issue that will detain us, however interesting it may be to New Testament scholarship.[2] The theologian works with the canonical presentation as God's gift to the church.

In Ephesians 4:30, Paul commands his readers not to grieve the Spirit. This is an extraordinary imperative. How can the Holy Spirit of God be grieved? As Thomas Weinandy points out, the majority opinion in theological discourse until late in the nineteenth century was that God, by definition, could not suffer.[3] Since then, the tra-

---

[1]D. A. Carson and Douglas J. Moo, *An Introduction to the New Testament*, 2nd ed. (Grand Rapids, MI: Zondervan; Leicester: Apollos, 2005), 488–90. The latter would be the case if his letter to the Ephesians was a more general one that was meant to be passed around and read by other congregations in the Lycus Valley.

[2]Increasingly critical New Testament scholarship regards the letter as written by a disciple of Paul rather than by Paul himself. For a discussion of the issues of authorship and especially arguments in favor of its authenticity, see ibid., 480–86.

[3]Thomas G. Weinandy, "Does God Suffer?" *First Things*, 117 (November 2001), 35. Also see

ditional view has gone somewhat into eclipse. Biblical speech about apparent divine suffering is a manner of speaking that needs special care in interpreting correctly. As we shall see, Luther, Calvin, and Owen took the traditional approach. However, is it a sound one? If not, how then are we to think of God suffering?

Theological reflection not only asks the normative questions, "What ought we to believe?" and "How ought we to live?" Such reflection also asks, "What follows if such and such is the case?" With regard to our present focus the question becomes, then, "What, if anything, follows for our doctrine of God if special revelation discloses that the Holy Spirit may be grieved? Does the living God really have something analogous to human emotional life?"

We will begin with how grieving the Holy Spirit has been understood in the past as well as present perspectives. Next we will engage the biblical testimony before offering a theological reflection. Our question is not an esoteric one. As we shall see, for the evangelical, the evangelistic must not be divorced from the ethical. Otherwise, the Spirit is grieved.

GRIEVING THE SPIRIT:
SOME PAST AND PRESENT PERSPECTIVES

We start with Calvin. Ephesians was his favorite apostolic letter.[4] In his commentary on Ephesians 4:30, Calvin argues:

> As the Holy Spirit dwells in us, to him every part of our soul and of our body ought to be devoted. But if we give ourselves unto aught that is impure, we may be said to drive him away from making his abode with us; and, to express this still more familiarly, human affections, such as joy and grief, are ascribed to the Holy Spirit. Endeavour that the Holy Spirit may dwell cheerfully with you, as in a pleasant and joyful dwelling, and give him no occasion for grief.[5]

But how do we give the Spirit grief? Calvin answers:

his, *Does God Suffer?* (Edinburgh: T. and T. Clark, 2000).
[4]Max Turner, "Ephesians, Book of," ed. Kevin J. Vanhoozer, *Dictionary for Theological Interpretation of the Bible* (London: SPCK; Grand Rapids, MI: Baker Books, 2005), 186.
[5]John Calvin, *CJCC*, comment on Eph. 4:30.

> As God has sealed us by his Spirit, we grieve him when we do not
> follow his guidance, but pollute ourselves by wicked passions. No
> language can adequately express this solemn truth, that the Holy
> Spirit rejoices and is glad on our account, when we are obedient to
> him in all things, and neither think nor speak anything, but what is
> pure and holy; and, on the other hand, is grieved, when we admit
> anything into our minds that is unworthy of our calling.[6]

Furthermore, Calvin suggests that in so grieving the Spirit by "shocking
wickedness," we might in fact "compel him to withdraw from us."[7]

I have quoted Calvin's comment *in extenso* because he writes
with such clarity. According to the sixteenth-century Reformer, our
moral conduct will either grieve or please the Spirit. The question,
however, is just how does Calvin understand this Pauline language
theologically? He acknowledges that behind Paul's words stands the
prophet Isaiah, who similarly spoke of grieving the Spirit. Calvin
writes: "The same mode of speaking is used by the prophet Isaiah,
but in a different sense; for he merely says, that they 'vexed his Holy
Spirit,' in the same sense in which we are accustomed to speak of
vexing the mind of a man."

Calvin's commentary on Isaiah 63:10 provides further insight
into his understanding of our Pauline text. In it Calvin specifically
refers to Ephesians 4:30. He says: "We are said to irritate 'the Holy
Spirit' by our wickedness; and this form of expression, after the
manner of men, is intended to produce in us stronger abhorrence
against sin, which provokes God's wrath and hatred."[8] The key
phrase is "after the manner of men." For Calvin, both the prophet
and the apostle in speaking of the grief of the Spirit are offering an
anthropopathism. That is to say, God is spoken of as having human
emotion. However, theologically understood, God does not. Rather,
from the perspective of the prophet and the apostle, God appears to
have grief, but in fact by definition does not. We ascribe to God the
grief at sin that we ought to feel.

---

[6]Ibid.
[7]Ibid. Calvin does not connect this idea of the Spirit's withdrawal with the idea of the unpardonable sin. However, some have connected Eph. 4:30 and the unpardonable sin. But this sees a nexus
of which the New Testament writings are innocent. See James F. Holladay Jr., "Ephesians 4:30: Do
Not Grieve the Spirit," *Review and Expositor*, 94 (1997), 81–87.
[8]Calvin, *CJCC*, comment on Isa. 63:10.

Calvin was not only a commentary writer, he was also a preacher, and his sermon on Ephesians 4:29–30 is even bolder than his commentary on the point that we are considering:

> For we know that there are no passions in God. It is the property of men to be grieved and offended. God is unchangeable. Nevertheless, because we do not conceive that he is most high, and that his majesty is so infinite that we cannot approach it, the apostle therefore uses a comparison, even for the sake of our ignorance. . . . The Scripture then does not mean to make God subject to any change, when it says that he is angry or is grieved, but it leads us to our own doings, in order that our vices should grieve us so much more, and that we should abhor them.[9]

Calvin's exegesis is controlled by a belief brought to the text that God is infinite, unchanging, and passionless. Hence Paul's language about the Spirit cannot be accepted as it stands.

We are seeing Calvin's doctrine of accommodation at work. His commentary on Genesis 6:6 with its reference to God's repentance and grief states this idea of *accommodatio* clearly:

> The repentance which is here ascribed to God does not properly belong to him, but has reference to our understanding of him. For since we cannot comprehend him as he is, it is necessary that, for our sakes he should, in a certain sense, transform himself. That repentance cannot take place in God, easily appears from this single consideration that nothing happens which is by him unexpected or unforeseen. The same reasoning, and remark, applies to what follows, that God was affected with grief.
>
> Certainly God is not sorrowful or sad; but remains forever like himself in his celestial and happy repose: yet, because it could not otherwise be known how great is God's hatred and detestation of sin, therefore the Spirit accommodates himself to our capacity.[10]

Like an expert rhetorician, God stoops to the audience's level in order to communicate to us his will and his ways.[11]

Interestingly, Martin Luther took a similar interpretive line with regard to Genesis 6:6, which states: "The Lord was sorry that

---

[9]John Calvin, *Sermons on the Epistle to the Ephesians* (London: 1973), 467.
[10]John Calvin, *CJCC*, comment on Gen. 6:6.
[11]Ford Lewis Battles, "God Was Accommodating Himself to Human Capacity," *Interpretation* 31 (January 1977): 19–38.

he made man on the earth and it grieved him to his heart." In his commentary on Genesis 6:6 he wrote: "One should not imagine that God has a heart or that He can grieve. But when the spirit of Noah, Lamech, and of Methuselah is grieved, God himself is said to be grieved. Thus we should understand this grief to refer to its effect, not to the divine essence."[12] In other words, on analysis the biblical testimony is not about God, but about us, and the effects that divine action produces in us.

In the century after Calvin, John Owen argued that the soul may deport itself in "three general ways" in its communion with the Holy Spirit.[13] The Scripture presents these ways in negative terms. As we saw in our previous study, Owen maintained that with regard to the Spirit's "actings and motions of his grace" we may quench him. According to Owen we resist the Spirit when we disobey the Word of God. However, in grieving the Spirit we, in a manner of speaking, make sorrowful the person of the Spirit who indwells the believer.[14]

With regard to the language of grief when predicated of the Spirit, Owen argued in a way similar to Calvin. Owen contends that:

> The Spirit cannot be grieved, or affected with sorrow; which infers alteration, disappointment, weakness—all incompatible with his infinite perfections; yet men may actively do that which is fit and able to grieve any one that stands affected towards them as doth the Holy Ghost. If he be not grieved, it is no thanks to us, but to his unchangeable nature.[15]

To speak of the Spirit's grief is to speak of how the Spirit "is affected towards us." It is to speak as "if he were grieved as we are."[16] According to Owen: "Such affections and perturbations of mind are not ascribed unto God or the Spirit but metaphorically."[17]

[12]Jaroslav Pelikan, ed., *Luther's Works* (St. Louis, MO: Concordia, 1955), 2:49.
[13]William H. Goold, ed., *The Works of John Owen*, vol. 2 (Edinburgh: Banner of Truth Trust, 1980), 264.
[14]Ibid.
[15]Ibid., 265.
[16]Ibid.
[17]John Owen, *Pneumatologia* (London: 1674), with reference to Gen. 6:6 and like Scriptures, http://www.ccel.org/owen/pneumhtm (accessed April 23, 2006).

Both Calvin and Owen stand in what is described as the classical theistic tradition. In this tradition it is axiomatic that God by definition, in order to be the most perfect being, is impassible in both the general and particular senses of the word. In general terms, he cannot be acted on without his free consent and in particular terms, he cannot suffer in any sense. But are Calvin and Owen right on this point?

J. I. Packer would suggest that Calvin and Owen—and he admires both immensely—and the classical theistic tradition have not understood such biblical references to God's grief aright. This is one area of theistic thought where the tradition needs "retooling." He acknowledges that Scripture presents anthropomorphisms ("phrases using human figures to describe God"). This phenomenon of language, however, is entirely appropriate since we are created in the divine image. He argues that the notion of God's impassibility "was introduced into Christian theology in the second century." He maintains:

> Let us be clear: A totally impassive God would be a horror, and not the God of Calvary at all. He might belong in Islam; he has no place in Christianity. If, therefore, we can learn to think of the *chosenness* of God's grief and pain as the essence of his impassibility, so-called, we will do well.[18]

If Packer is right, then Calvin and Owen stand corrected. Who then has the better of the argument? We will need to return to this question at a later stage. Much hangs on our answer. Before we do, however, we need to ask what Paul actually meant when he wrote of grieving the Spirit.

THE BIBLICAL TESTIMONY

Structurally speaking, Paul's command not to grieve the Spirit falls into that part of Ephesians dealing with the lifestyle that comports with God's call for unity (Eph. 4:1–3). There is one body, one Spirit, one hope, one Lord, one faith, one baptism, one God and Father of

---

[18]J. I. Packer, "What Do You Mean When You Say 'God'?" *Christianity Today,* September 19, 1986, 27–31 (original emphasis). Packer is not commenting specifically on Eph. 4:30. However, *mutatis mutandis* his remarks would apply to this text.

all (Eph. 4:4–6). Indeed, the ascended Christ bestows his gifts for ministry with the aim of creating one new man whose head is Christ (Eph. 4:7–16). To live in ways that are in keeping with this new reality means putting off the characteristics of the former life and putting on, like a new set of clothing, the defining characteristics of the new one (Eph. 4:17–29). It is against that backdrop that the Holy Spirit of God is not to be grieved (Eph. 4:30). After all, either it is the Spirit who is the authenticating stamp, as it were, that we belong to God and that God's future for us will be realized, or, perhaps, it is the Spirit who stamps us to the same effect.

Paul does not elaborate on what grieving the Spirit precisely means, but the context makes it plain that our moral life is the key. In negative terms we grieve the Spirit by lying, giving place to the devil, stealing, speaking corruptly, showing bitterness, wrath, anger, clamor, and malice (Eph. 4:25–31). In positive terms we do not grieve the Spirit when we speak truth with our neighbor, are angry but do not sin with it, work and use the product of our labor to do good to the needy, use speech to edify and impart grace to our hearers, are kind, tenderhearted, and forgiving (Eph. 4:25–32). The word translated grieve is *lypeō* and covers a range of meanings, including grieve, suffer pain, and suffer injury.[19] Paul's first letter to the Thessalonians provides an example of its use as Paul counsels the Thessalonians not to grieve over the death of a loved one, as though they had no Christian hope (1 Thess. 4:13).[20] Paul has sadness in mind. Similarly he has sadness in view when he writes to those troublesome Corinthians, informing them in his second letter that he had determined not to come to them in sorrow or to make them sorrowful. What Paul wants instead is joy (2 Cor. 4:2–5, with its use of a mix of *lypeō* and *lypē*). The argument, that grieving the Spirit is offending the Spirit and therefore runs the risk of losing

---

[19]The verb *lypeō* is used of "to distress, to grieve, to cause pain or grief" (e.g., Matt. 14:9; 17:23; 18:31; 19:22; 26:22; Mark 10:22; 14:9; John 16:20; 21:17; Rom. 14:15; 2 Cor. 2:4; 6:10; 7:9, 11; 1 Thess. 4:13; 1 Pet. 1:6; as well as Eph. 4:30). See G. Abbott-Smith, *A Manual Greek Lexicon of the New Testament*, 3rd ed. (Edinburgh: T. and T. Clark, 1968), 272.

[20]Many commentators have seen in Eph. 4:30 a clear allusion to Isa. 63:10. However, a different Greek word is used in the LXX version of Isa. 63:10 (*paroxynō*: to provoke, to stimulate, to irritate). Paul's use of the full descriptor The Holy Spirit of God, though, does point to a deliberate allusion to Isa. 63:10 with Paul correcting the LXX rendering of the Hebrew. See the discussion in Gordon D. Fee, *God's Empowering Presence: The Holy Spirit in the Letters of Paul* (Peabody, MA: Hendrickson, 2005), 713, fn. 175.

the Spirit, may have support in early church commentary, but not
in the Pauline text.[21]

If we claim to be Christian, yet live as though Christ had never
come, then we grieve the Spirit, but if we live as though he has
indeed really come and we truly belong to him, then we do not
grieve the Spirit. Instead we exhibit the true righteousness and holiness that should characterize the restored images of God that we are
in process of becoming (Eph. 4:23–24). Such images should indeed
imitate God, as Paul goes on to argue (Eph. 5:1).

Importantly, the context is communal. Paul is concerned with
maintaining the unity of the Spirit. As Gordon Fee rightly argues:
"Life in Christ means to live the life of God in the context of 'one
another' (v. 32)."[22] How we behave in relation to one another is the
crucial part of the story of not grieving the Spirit. As Max Turner
suggests, the horizontal dimension of Christian community, as well
as the vertical one of communion with God in Christ by the Spirit,
is integral to the presentation of the letter to the Ephesians, which
has been described as the "crown of Paulinism."[23]

THEOLOGICAL REFLECTION

As we reflect theologically on this Pauline command, we begin with
considering what import it has for our doctrine of God, in particular
whether God suffers and whether the Holy Spirit is truly personal.
Lastly, we shall consider how we ought to live in the light of this
imperative.

Does God the Holy Spirit Suffer?

As we saw earlier, Owen and Calvin thought not. The Pauline text is
an anthropopathism. The text is about us and how sinful attitudes
and actions ought to grieve us. The Spirit as God is by definition

---

[21]This is the argument found in early church literature, beginning with the *Shepherd of Hermas.*
See Dennis W. Johnson, *Grieving and Quenching the Holy Spirit* (Trinity Evangelical Divinity
School, 1993), unpublished MA thesis, 12. Johnson understands Eph. 4:30 as referring to "the
outrage and indignation of a king who discovers a traitor among his most loyal subjects," ibid.,
129. However, comparing 2 Cor. 2:2–5, 1 Thess. 4:13, and Eph. 4:30 makes his suggestion most
unlikely.
[22]Fee, *Presence*, 713.
[23]Turner, "Ephesians," 189–90.

impassible in every sense of the word. Packer has problems with this classical theistic view. Scripture that is ostensibly about God is in fact about us. He writes:

> ... to say that some things that Scripture affirms about God do not mean what they seem to mean, and do mean what they do not seem to mean. That provokes the question: How can these statements be part of the *revelation* of God when they actually *misrepresent and so conceal* God?[24]

His point is well taken. If the language of grief is only a manner of speaking, then why stop there? Why not treat the biblical language about God's love and God's wrath the same way?

The way forward is to make a theological distinction. God is spirit (John 4:24). Consequently, biblical language that describes God as having a human form is clearly metaphorical: God's eyes, ears, nostrils, finger, arm, and so forth. God's hand speaks in context of God's strength and power: "The Lord's hand is not shortened, that it cannot save" (Isa. 59:1). This is anthropomorphism, part of the accommodation of God to our capacity to comprehend that communicative action we call special revelation.[25] But anthropopathism refers to the ascription to God of an emotional life like our own—albeit without the warping effects of sin, living as we do outside Eden. There is no obvious contradiction in predicating emotions of God who is spirit. For this reason and given the biblical testimonies, Packer's retooling of the tradition itself is in need of retooling. He makes God's grief the result of a divine choice. "Chosenness" is his term. He appears to want to preserve the freedom of God to relate to us as he so wishes. However, is this move necessary? I think not, as long as the distinction between biblical anthropomorphisms and biblical anthropopathisms is carefully observed.[26]

The question may be raised, however, whether ascribing emo-

---

[24]J. I. Packer, "What Do You Mean When You Say 'God'?" 30 (original emphasis).
[25]For a helpful discussion of communicative action, see Kevin J. Vanhoozer, *First Theology: God, Scripture and Hermeneutics* (Downers Grove, IL: InterVarsity; Leicester: Apollos, 2002), 159–203.
[26]See my, "The Living God: Anthropomorphic or Anthropopathic?" *Reformed Theological Review*, 59 (1, 2000).

tion to God contravenes classic Christian statements such as Article 1 of the Thirty-Nine Articles, which declares, "There is but one living and true God, everlasting, without body, parts, or passions." Depends. Everything hangs on what is meant by "passions." If having passions means being prone to emotional mood swings and irrational actions, rushes of divine blood as it were, then, no. But God may be passionate without having passions in the deleterious sense. That is to say, God's commitments are expressions of a constancy of moral character that has dependable feeling-like tones. The God of the theophany on Sinai who declared his name to Moses is gracious and merciful, slow to anger, and abounding in steadfast love, and by no means condones evil (Ex. 34:6–7). Bible story after Bible story gives narrative shape to this declaration, culminating in the saving career of Christ and the cross.

In the early church period, Tertullian (c. A.D. 160–c. 225) made a useful distinction between emotions (*motus* and *sensus*) and passions (*passiones*). God has emotions and feelings as we do, but not those passions in us that subvert our moral character.[27] Indeed, for some early church figures the scriptural testimony to a passionate God was one clear indicator that the God of the scriptural revelation was not like the unfeeling deities of paganism (e.g., Lactantius and Gregory Thaumaturgus).[28]

Significantly, the most able defender of the impassibility of God in present times, Thomas Weinandy, is comfortable with speaking of God as passionate but not driven by changeable passions. He writes: "God is impassible in that He does not undergo successive and fluctuating emotional states, nor can the created order alter Him in such a way as to cause Him to suffer any modification or loss."[29] However, he also writes: "God is absolutely impassible because He is absolutely passionate in His love."[30] Weinandy's argument is that God by definition cannot become more loving than he is or

---

[27]See E. Evans, ed. and trans., *Tertullian Adversus Marcionem* (London: Oxford University Press, 1972), 129–33; and my "Living God," fn. 23.
[28]Marcel Sarot, "'Does God Suffer?' A Critical Discussion of Thomas Weinandy's 'Does God Suffer?'" http://www.arsdisutandi.org/publish/ articles/000018/article.htm (accessed October 11, 2005).
[29]Weinandy, "Does God Suffer?"
[30]Ibid.

less loving than he is. Therefore he is impassible in the sense that he does not change. He is even prepared to say that God "does grieve over sin."[31] On this view, when we see Scripture present a God who on occasion is angry towards his people, that is no indicator that the divine emotional state has fluctuated from love to wrath. Rather God's constant love shows itself as mercy on occasion and God's constant holiness shows itself as wrath on other occasions. The key is that mercy and wrath presuppose a creation that has gone wrong. However, God as Trinity has always been loving and holy with or without a creation. Love and holiness are essential attributes of God, whereas mercy and wrath are contingent characteristics of God: contingent upon the divine decision to create and permit the fall. Like Packer, then, Weinandy has retooled classical theism, but does not seem to see that he has done so.

The so-called apathy axiom, which argues that God by definition cannot suffer, has had a long history in philosophical discourse. According to Sextus Empiricus, the second-century philosopher, it was "the dogma of the philosophers that the Deity is impassible."[32] In religion it was Philo of Alexandria (c. 20 b.c.–c. a.d. 50) who argued that in the Torah, where emotions like suffering are attributed to God, what is being portrayed are not affects in God but effects in us.[33] Marcel Sarot argues that for Philo: "*we* experience God's unchanging and unfailing love now as blissful, then as suffering, and then as repentance, because of changes in *us*."[34] This idea of divine impassibility entered the Christian bloodstream in the second century, particularly through writers such as Clement of Alexandria.[35] The "apathy axiom" became fundamental to classical theism. In my view, however, Paul's command not to grieve the

---

[31]Ibid.

[32]Quoted in Abraham J. Heschel, *The Prophets*, vol. 2 (New York: Harper and Row, 1962), 42.

[33]Richard J. Gibson, As *Dearly Loved Children: Divine and Human Emotion in Early Christian Thought and Its Hellenistic Context* (Macquarie University, 2005), unpublished doctoral thesis, 422.

[34]Sarot, "Does God Suffer?" (original emphases). Also see his "Patripassianism, Theopaschitism and the Suffering of God. Some Historical and Systematic Considerations," *Religious Studies* 26 (1990), 363–75.

[35]Gibson, *As Dearly Loved Children*, 424. Paul Gavilyuk goes too far in his attempt to debunk "the theory of theology's fall into Hellenistic philosophy," *The Suffering of the Impassible God: The Dialectics of Patristic Thought* (Oxford: Oxford University Press, 2004), 1.

Holy Spirit exposes the Achilles heel of classical theism and its need for retooling.[36]

A great theologian of the past who appreciated the need to rethink our inherited theology in the light of the biblical testimony was B. B. Warfield (1851–1921). In one of his sermons he proclaimed:

> Men tell us that God is, by very necessity of His nature, incapable of passion, incapable of being moved by inducements from without; that he dwells in holy calm [the apathy axiom] and unchangeable blessedness, untouched by human suffering or sorrows. . . . Let us bless our God that it is not true. God can feel; God does love.[37]

He then adds with rhetorical flourish:

> But is not this gross anthropomorphism [more precisely anthropopathism]? We are careless of names; it is the truth of God. And we decline to yield up the God of the Bible and the God of our hearts to any philosophical abstraction.[38]

In this post-Holocaust, post-arrival-of-AIDS, post-9/11 world, we need to hear this afresh. The Spirit may be grieved. Our God is not an immobile absolute, indifferent to feeling and emotion.

A further point: if the Spirit can really be grieved, then the Holy Spirit is truly personal. Some of the biblical symbols of the Spirit, if considered in isolation from texts like Ephesians 4:30, might suggest that the Spirit is impersonal: dove (Mark 1:11), water (John 7:37–39), wind (John 3:8), breath (Ps. 104:29), oil (Luke 4:18),

---

[36]Retooling classical theism does not entail embracing open theism with its attenuated understanding of divine omniscience. However, open theism has done a service in putting the question of the nature of biblical anthropomorphisms and anthropopathisms on the theologian's agenda in a challenging way.

[37]B. B. Warfield, *The Person and Work of Christ* (Philadelphia: Presbyterian and Reformed, 1950), 570. Warfield's sermon is based on Phil. 2:5–11, but applies *mutatis mutandis* to Eph. 4:30. Paul Gavilyuk argues that such a vision makes the incarnation superfluous, since God already knows suffering on this view, *The Suffering of the Impassible God*, 20. However, Gavilyuk does not reckon with the idea that although God knows all true propositions about human suffering and that they are true and all false propositions about human suffering and that they are false, without the incarnation God the Son does not know what it is to weep a human tear. The incarnation is not rendered superfluous by the notion of a God who may suffer.

[38]Warfield, ibid. Warfield knew great personal suffering in his life because of the chronic illness of his wife. This may account for his passion. See M. A. Noll, "B. B. Warfield" in ed. W. E. Elwell, *Handbook of Evangelical Theologians* (Grand Rapids, MI: Baker Books, 1993), 27.

fire (Acts 2:3), and fruit tree (Gal. 5:22).[39] However, a mere divine influence or force can hardly be grieved.

Evangelical and Ethical

We grieve the Spirit when our espoused theology (what we say we believe) and our operational theology (how we actually behave) stand in moral contradiction. Evangelicalism in recent centuries has been extremely strong on Galatians 2:20, recognizing that the love of Christ is directed at the individual. However, has evangelicalism been equally strong on Ephesians 5:25 and recognized that Christ loved the church and gave himself for her? I say "in recent centuries" because, as Mark Noll points out: "Up to the early 1700s, British Protestants preached on God's plan *for the church*. From the mid-1700s, however, evangelicals emphasized God's plans *for the individual*."[40] Sadly, a deep appreciation of ecclesiology has not usually been regarded as a modern evangelical strength.[41] However, in Pauline perspective, both the one and the many matter to God. We grieve the Spirit when we do not recognize one another as fellow members of the body of Christ, or, to change the Pauline image, as parts together of the temple of the Spirit. Community in character, as Stanley Hauerwas happily expresses it.[42] Our lived ecclesiology is of profound importance.

Lack of moral integrity grieves the Spirit, who is after all the *Holy* Spirit. For example, the evangelistic—a strength of evangelicalism as a movement—must not be divorced from the ethical. Again Paul did not divorce the two. He spent three weeks at Thessalonica, and yet he left them not only an evangel (1 Thess. 1:9–10) but also an ethic: "You received from us how you ought to live and to please God" (1 Thess. 4:1–8). However, there is a kind

[39]See the discussion in Edwin H. Palmer, *The Holy Spirit*, rev. ed. (Philadelphia: Presbyterian and Reformed, 1971), 153–63.

[40]Mark Noll, "Father of Modern Evangelicals," *Christian History* (Spring 1993): 44 (original emphases).

[41]J. I. Packer rightly notes that there was a time when "Protestants . . . were always careful to set personal religion in a communal, ecclesiastical frame," ibid. An earlier contribution to pneumatology by Packer preserves the balance. See A. M. Stibbs and J. I. Packer, *The Spirit within You: The Church's Neglected Possession* (London: Hodder and Stoughton, 1967).

[42]Stanley Hauerwas, *A Community of Character: Toward a Constructive Christian Social Ethic* (Notre Dame, IN: University of Notre Dame Press, 1981). The title is eloquent.

of gospel consequentialism that I have observed in some circles. If there is a good gospel outcome arising from a course of action, then the action is morally justified. By "a good gospel outcome" I mean that as a result of an action people get to hear the gospel and/ or are converted to Christ. God, however, in biblical perspective is interested in the moral agent (as in 2 Peter 1), the moral action (as in Exodus 20) and the moral aftermath (as in Proverbs).

I recall as a new Christian wanting to learn how to do public evangelism. I am sure I was motivated in part at least by the fact that I had come to faith in Christ through such evangelism. I attended a variety of evangelistic events in order to learn. One such stands out in my memory. The event took place in the open air and at night. The venue was a natural amphitheatre. The evangelist finished his talk and then invited all present to bow their heads in an attitude of prayer. He challenged us that if God had spoken to our hearts then we needed to raise our hands to accept Christ. I was at the very back, eyes open and surveying the entire scene. No hands were raised. Time was passing. More exhortations. The evangelist started thanking people for raising their hands: "Bless you, young man. I see your hand." "Thank you, young lady." The problem was that no hands had been raised. However, soon they were. How is such a practice justified, except by the ends justifying the means? This was not so much the triumph of the Holy Spirit, as it was that of Jeremy Bentham, the father of modern consequentialism.

A further example is in order. The previous one concerned believers and those on the outside. This one has to do with life in the body of Christ and the temple of the Spirit. A young man goes on the mission field. He is financially and prayerfully supported by his local church. He marries someone from the culture to which he has been sent and they begin to raise a family together. However, he has a same-sex affair. He repents and is deeply remorseful. He has betrayed his wife, his receiving and sending churches, and his Lord. He resigns and returns home. He confesses his sin to the send-ing church and shows the marks of real repentance. He asks for forgiveness. The leadership of the church, acting on behalf of the congregation, publicly forgive him. They then show him the door. He is never welcomed back.

The ethical can be unhinged from the evangelical and replaced by a "gospel" pragmatism. If there is a good ministry outcome or a good gospel outcome, then *how* we got to that point had to be right. We can be culturally captive to the consequentialist ethic of much of modern society and business, whereas the New Testament is much more interested in a Spirit-animated community that exhibits the moral character of a holy and loving God. The ethical can also be unhinged from the evangelical when we forget that we are a forgiven people and can no longer pray with integrity "forgive us our sins as we forgive those who sin against us."

CONCLUSION

Grieving the Spirit can be a sad reality of both Christian corporate and individual life. This Pauline idea is not to be explained away as a mere anthropopathism. If Scripture putatively speaking of God is actually speaking of ourselves, then we are left in deep agnosticism about the true nature of God. However, if we observe the distinction between an anthropomorphism and an anthropopathism, we need not refrain from ascribing something analogous to our emotional life to God. We grieve the Spirit when there is moral disparity between what we say as God's people and what we do. I say "we" in the first instance because the command is addressed to a congregation and not to an individual. How we relate to one another in the body of Christ and in the temple of the Spirit really does matter to God.

chapter six

HOW DOES THE
HOLY SPIRIT FILL US?

AMONGST OTHER QUESTIONS, thus far we have looked at whether we ought to pray to the Spirit, what it means to grieve the Spirit, and how we might quench the Spirit. None of these questions has had much theological attention, especially in recent times, compared to the question to which we now turn. The rise of Pentecostalism and then of the charismatic movement has put the question front and center with a host of others: the baptism with the Spirit, charismatic gifts, spiritual warfare, and the like. Given this attention, our focus on the Spirit's ministry in this last chapter will need to be narrower to make the discussion manageable—namely, "In the light of Paul's command to the Ephesians, 'Be filled with or by the Spirit,' how does the Spirit fill us?"

As in our previous studies, we begin by looking at what has been said in the past and what our contemporaries are saying. To this end I will concentrate on Calvin as the representative of the past and John Stott for the present. Next we turn to the scriptural testimony before moving to theological reflection. Engaging the scriptural text confronts us with the question: "What does Scripture say?" (the biblical meaning question), while theological reflection raises

the question, "So what?" (the theological significance question).
It is one thing to describe as accurately as one can what Scripture
presents; it is quite another task to know what to do with it. That is
especially where our theology kicks in.

THE COMMAND TO BE FILLED BY THE SPIRIT: SOME PAST AND PRESENT PERSPECTIVES

For a perspective from the past we turn to Calvin. Calvin has surprisingly little to say about the command in his commentary on
Ephesians. He notes the contrast between "excessive and immoder-
ate drinking of every description," which the apostle forbids, and
the "exhortation" to "deep drinking" with regard to the Spirit. The
problem with drinking to excess is the immorality to which it leads.
As for the reference to the Spirit, he seems to understand this as a
way of speaking about "joy in the holy Ghost."[1] As in so many
other of his commentaries, when Calvin comments on texts referring to the fullness of the Spirit, there is very little discussion of the
idea per se (e.g., his commentary on Acts).

Calvin is more expansive on the subject of the Ephesians' command in his sermon on Ephesians 5:18–21. He contrasts being full
of wine and being full of the Spirit's gifts. People full of wine "break
out into all kinds of wickedness, so that they are past all shame, and
yet men ought to be filled with loathing to see their depravity—
when that happens the mischief is increased so much the more."[2]
To be filled with the Spirit, however, is to be filled with "faith,"
"the fear of God," and "joy." He preaches: "For if we were once
well filled with such meats, it is certain that we would not act like
wolves in devouring, but would keep ourselves within bounds. That
then is the reason why St Paul says that we must be filled with the
Holy Spirit."[3] We must come to hear the Word hungry to be filled,
he argues. His exhortation is that we are to "fill ourselves fearlessly
with the gifts of God's Spirit, and with his spiritual benefits."[4] Yet

---

[1]John Calvin, *CJCC*, comment on Eph. 5:18.
[2]John Calvin, *Sermons on the Epistle to the Ephesians* (Edinburgh: Banner of Truth Trust, 1979), 549.
[3]Ibid., 550.
[4]Ibid.

this filling is a concursive activity. It is the Spirit who is in fact feeding our hunger by these gifts and spiritual benefits.[5] Clearly, for Calvin, to be full of the Spirit is not to be full of the Spirit per se so much as to be full of what the Spirit is willing to give the spiritually famished child of God.

Our contemporary figure is John Stott. In his classic book *Baptism and Fullness: The Work of the Holy Spirit Today* he devotes an entire chapter to the subject of the fullness of the Spirit. In this discussion he first distinguishes the idea of the baptism of the Spirit, which he regards as an initial gospel blessing that is given to all Christians, and the fullness of the Spirit, which he maintains is a "gift [that] needs to be *continuously and increasingly appropriated.*"[6] In his view, the New Testament implies that the fullness of the Spirit "was a normal characteristic of every dedicated Christian."[7] He acknowledges that Ephesians 5:18 is the only biblical place where there is a command to be filled. As one might expect of Stott, he is soon into the Greek. From the Greek of Ephesians 5:18–21 he argues that obedience to the command to be filled with the Spirit results in four marks of fullness: "speaking" to one another, "singing and making melody," "giving thanks," and "submitting." These participles depend upon the verb "to be filled." In contrast to drunkenness, fullness of the Spirit is about a different kind of control over behavior. The Spirit's control does not lead to "unrestrained and irrational licence," but to transformation into the image of Christ.[8]

The results of the Spirit's fullness are relational. Two of the results concern our relationship to God: "singing and making melody to the Lord" and "giving thanks." There is a vertical dimension. The other two are horizontal in direction: "speaking" to each other and "submitting" to one another. The last idea is controversial as a number of translations will show (e.g., NRSV). A number of commentators link the idea of submission to what follows concerning

[5]Ibid.
[6]John R. W. Stott, *Baptism and Fullness: The Work of the Holy Spirit Today*, 2nd ed. (London: Inter-Varsity, 1975), 47 (original emphasis).
[7]Ibid., 48.
[8]Ibid., 54–59.

relations in the Christian household rather than to the fullness by the Spirit in congregational life.

Stott pays particular attention to the command to be filled. He correctly points out that the mood is imperative, the verb is plural, the voice is passive, and the tense—some would rather say "aspect"—is present continuous. The Spirit's fullness requires "continuous appropriation."[9] "Yes, but how?" one might ask. Stott's answer is somewhat vague. We are told that disbelief loses the Spirit's fullness. He exhorts the reader to "constantly seek to be filled with the Spirit."[10] Finally we are told that a condition of fullness is that we are to be hungry for it.

A small but widely used booklet, at least in the United States, has no reticence in specifying how the command is obeyed. How we breathe is used as an analogy of the process. We breathe out the bad air and then breathe in the good. (Of course, that depends a little bit on how close to a factory you might live.) Likewise, in spiritual terms, we confess our sins and thus breathe out the bad air, and we surrender afresh to the Spirit's control through prayer in obedience to Ephesians 5:18 and thus breathe in the good air of the Spirit. This spiritual breathing ought to be the normal Christian life if we are to be fruitful and contented in the service of God. Indeed, we are told that "every day can be an exciting adventure for the Christian."[11] One wonders how such sanguinity comports with Paul's depression, anxiety, and burdens, which he so candidly shares in 2 Corinthians.

The question is, however, whether Scripture supports these contentions.

THE BIBLICAL TESTIMONY

The New Testament accounts of the Spirit empowering God's people are of such a number that Gordon Fee sums up the Pauline view of the Spirit, for example, as "God's empowering presence." Of course, God's empowerment of his people has

[9]Ibid., 60–61.
[10]Ibid., 75.
[11]"Have You Made the Wonderful Discovery of the Spirit-Filled Life?" http://www.greatcom.org/spirit/english (accessed April 23, 2006).

had a long history before Pentecost. Leaders like Moses knew that empowerment, as did prophets like Elijah and Elisha and kings like David. Indeed, in the four canonical Gospels we see such empowerment at work in John the Baptist and, supremely, in Jesus. To understand the nature of Spirit empowerment let us briefly explore the nature of the filling of the Spirit, post-Pentecost especially.

Like Stott, it seems to me that a distinction needs to be made between the baptism of the Spirit as conversion-initiation and fullness of the Spirit for empowerment.[12] On the day of Pentecost, those, like Peter, who experienced the tongues of fire were subject to both. Over and over again in Luke–Acts we read of those filled with the Spirit. Importantly this expression is often followed by or follows the conjunction "and" (an observation I owe to my theological teacher, D. B. Knox).[13] For example, even before Pentecost and right at the start of Luke we find that John the Baptist will be filled with the Spirit *and* will turn many to the Lord (Luke 1:15–16). Elizabeth was filled with the Holy Spirit *and* exclaimed a blessing upon Mary (Luke 1:41–42). Again, Zechariah was filled with the Holy Spirit *and* prophesied (Luke 1:67). Similarly in Acts, we read of those gathered together on the day of Pentecost that they were filled with the Spirit *and* spoke in other tongues (Acts 2:4). Some time later, as the Acts narrative unfolds, the believers, in a context of hostility, were filled with the Holy Spirit *and* continued to speak the Word of God (the gospel) with boldness (Acts 4:31). Paul, when confronting Elymas the magician at Paphos, was filled with the Holy Spirit *and* pronounced a rebuke (Acts 13:9–10). These instances of filling are conjoined with some kind of speech act.

Another kind of conjunction found in Acts is where the filling of the Spirit is conjoined to some aspect of character or personal

---

[12]This distinction is well articulated and defended by Andreas J. Köstenberger, "What Does It Mean to Be Filled with the Holy Spirit? A Biblical Investigation," *JETS* 40/2 (June 1997): 229–40, especially 236, fn. 27; also see D. A. Carson, *Showing the Spirit* (Grand Rapids, MI: Baker Books, 1987), 158–60.

[13]See the valuable discussion of this phenomenon by D. Broughton Knox in, *D. Broughton Knox Selected Works Volume 1: The Doctrine of God*, ed. Tony Payne (Kingsford, NSW: Matthias Media, 2000), 271–72. I am very much indebted to Knox for this paragraph.

life.[14] And so we read of the seven, who were sought to relieve the apostles from table duty, that they were to be full of the Spirit *and* wisdom (Acts 6:3). One of them is singled out. The narrative goes on to present Stephen as full of faith *and* the Holy Spirit (Acts 6:5). At a later stage in the narrative Barnabas is described in the same terms: full of the Holy Spirit *and* faith (Acts 11:24). Further on still, the disciples are presented as full of the Holy Spirit *and* joy (Acts 13:52).[15]

Whether what is on view is the fullness of the Spirit and some action, or the fullness of the Spirit and some quality, there is no suggestion in these narratives that some kind of concursus was involved. That is to say, there is no hint that to be so filled was an intentionally cooperative activity involving the persons concerned and the Spirit of God. Instead these instances of fullness—both Old Testament and New—appear to have been the sovereign work of the Spirit.

In my view it is important to distinguish the kinds of fullness delineated above ("fullness and") from the kind of fullness of which Paul famously writes in Ephesians 5:18–21, which is our focus. This key passage bears quotation, reminding ourselves, as Stott well pointed out, that we are dealing with one long sentence in the Greek (correct in the ESV, but broken up in the NIV):

> And do not get drunk with wine, for that is debauchery, but be filled [continuously, imperative, 2nd person plural, present aspect of *plēroō*] with the Spirit [lit., in or by Spirit, *en pneumati*], addressing [*lalountes*, continuously, present participle] one another in psalms and hymns and spiritual songs, singing and making melody [continuously, both present participles, *adontes* and *psallontes*, respectively] to the Lord with all your heart, giving thanks

---

[14]Sinclair Ferguson observes that in Luke–Acts the *plēroō* family of words is used of the fruit of the Spirit (e.g., Luke 4:1; Acts 6:3) and the *pimplēmi* family of a special influx of ability and power in the service of the kingdom (e.g., Luke 1:41; Acts 2:4). See *The Holy Spirit* (Leicester: Inter-Varsity, 1996), 89. Also see G. Abbott-Smith, *A Manual Greek Lexicon of the New Testament*, 3rd ed. (Edinburgh: T. and T. Clark, 1968), 365 for *plēroō*, 360 for *pimplēmi*.

[15]Again, see Payne, ed., *Knox Selected Works*, vol. 1, 271–72. For another set of distinctions addressing the same textual phenomena, see Delbert R. Rose, "Distinguishing The Things That Differ," *Wesleyan Theological Journal*, vol. 9 (Spring 1974): 3–12. His categories are "charismatic fullness" (e.g., Luke 1:67), "ecstatic fullness" (e.g., Acts 13:52) and "ethical fullness" (e.g., Acts 15:8–9). These are Rose's examples. I prefer my adaptation of Knox's descriptors. The use of "charismatic" to describe the experience of John the Baptist and Zechariah, for example, I find somewhat confusing in the light of 1 Cor. 12–14.

[*eucharistountes*, continuously, present participle] always and for everything to God the Father in the name of our Lord Jesus Christ, submitting [*hypotassomenoi*, continuously, present participle] to one another out of reverence for Christ.[16]

We might call this "congregational fullness." On view is not the individual, but the congregation. And the fullness with the Spirit or by the Spirit concerns other-person-centered congregational activities as well as relating to God.[17] These are the sorts of activities that promote unity in the body of Christ, which is one of the great themes of Ephesians.

As we have seen, the traditional interpretation, as found in Calvin, Stott, and a host of others, is to argue that Paul is drawing a contrast between being under the sway of wine like the Gentiles and being under the sway of the Spirit. In the congregation, being under the sway of the Spirit shows in the practices found in Ephesians 5:19–21. Syntactically the participial phrases depend upon the filling as Stott argued. Paul commands the readers to be so filled continuously. If we follow the Knox line, then Paul is commanding that the Ephesians be filled with the Spirit *and* address one another in psalms and hymns and spiritual songs; be filled with the Spirit *and* sing and make melody to the Lord with all your heart; be filled with the Spirit *and* give thanks always and for everything to God the Father in the name of our Lord Jesus Christ; be filled with the Spirit *and* submit to one another out of reverence for Christ. It is, in other words, another example of "the Spirit-*and*" concept that we find elsewhere in the New Testament.

A newer view, however, maintains that Paul is commanding the readers to be filled by the Spirit with these practices and that these practices constitute the filling rather than the Holy Spirit per

---

[16]ESV with my additions. The NIV, however, breaks up the Greek into four English sentences. *En pneumati* has been taken by some commentators (e.g., Lenski) to mean the human spirit, but this is very unlikely given the other references to *pneuma* in Ephesians. Nor does the anarthrous use of *pneumati* point in that direction; see the discussion in Gordon Fee, *God's Empowering Presence: The Holy Spirit in the Letters of Paul* (Peabody, MA: Hendrickson, 2005), chap. 2.

[17]For a different view, see Wayne Grudem, *Systematic Theology: An Introduction to Biblical Doctrine* (Leicester: Inter-Varsity Press; Grand Rapids, MI: Zondervan, 1994), 781–84, who takes the traditional line that the passage is about the individual Christian and his or her increased sanctification and increased power for ministry.

se. On either view, the congregation is in mind, not individuals.[18] The Pauline command to be filled with or by the Spirit then is to be "understood in the context of Pauline ecclesiology rather than anthropology," as Andreas J. Köstenberger rightly argues.[19]

Moreover, on this more recent view, the contrast between drunk with wine as opposed to filled by the Spirit is to be regarded as a conventional one. Paul's point is about not living like pagans or meeting like pagans do. Some even suggest that Paul was in particular contrasting the sort of group behavior found in the Dionysian cult and which therefore ought not to characterize a Christian gathering.[20] On either view, Paul's argument is not so much about who is in control as it is about how to behave when gathered.

This approach has been well articulated by Timothy G. Gombis. He points out that relating the imperative of 5:18 to the five participles that follow in 5:19–21 is a vexing problem.[21] To solve it the whole epistle needs to be brought into the context for discussion. The earlier part of the epistle reveals that: "God has created the church to be his new temple, the place on earth where he dwells 'by the Spirit' (2:22)."[22] In that light, the corporate thrust of the command is clear. Furthermore, the contrast that Paul makes between the wine and the Spirit is one of a number in the second half of the letter between the old way of life and the new (e.g., light as opposed to darkness, wisdom as opposed to folly, and so forth). He argues that "the contrast in 5:18 between drunkenness and being filled by the Spirit is best understood against these 'two ways' of life."[23] A crucial part of his argument is that "it is preferable to read *en pneumati* as instrumental (i.e., 'filled *by* the Spirit')."[24] The various activities—speaking, singing, making melody, giving thanks and

---

[18]For a recent discussion of these two views (corporate versus individual), see Timothy G. Gombis, "Being the Fullness of God in Christ by the Spirit: Ephesians 5:18 in its Epistolary Setting," *TB* 53:2 (2002): 259–71. Gombis favors the "by the Spirit" view as we shall see.

[19]Köstenberger, "Filled with the Holy Spirit," 233–34.

[20]C. J. Rogers Jr., "The Dionysian Background of Ephesians 5:18," *BS* 136 (1979): 249–57, suggests the passage needs to be read against the backdrop of Dionysian reveling with its sexual and drunken debauchery. But it is hard to be this specific given the lack of detail in the text, as Gombis convincingly argues, "Fullness," 264, fn. 15.

[21]Gombis, "Fullness," 259.

[22]Ibid., 262.

[23]Ibid., 266.

[24]Ibid., 267 (original emphasis).

submitting—that depend upon the Spirit in our text are therefore "not best read as participles of result" so much as "participles of means."[25] In fact, it is as the church practices these activities that the command to be filled by the Spirit is obeyed. Gombis writes: "The five participles [activities] do not *lead to* the filling by the Spirit, rather they indicate *the means by which* the command is carried out."[26]

Since I will later follow this line of interpretation myself to see where it might lead theologically, I will not develop it any further at this point.

THEOLOGICAL REFLECTION

As we reflect theologically on the Pauline command, we shall pay particular attention to a methodological point, the command itself, and to the practicalities of being filled by the Spirit.

The Problem of a Unique Commandment

Richard B. Hays suggests a fourfold way forward in discovering how we are to live in the light of the biblical testimony. First, we endeavor to describe as accurately as we can what is in the text. This is the descriptive task. Next, we bring what we have discovered into relation with the rest of the biblical testimony. This is the synthetic task and, I might add, it is also the bread-and-butter work of the discipline of biblical theology. That is to say, the text is to be placed in its context in its argument in its literary genre in its book in the canon in the light of the flow of salvation history. Then, we attempt to relate what we have uncovered through carrying out the previous two tasks to the world in which we live. This is the hermeneutical task. The text and today need to be bridged. Finally, we make a decision as to how we are to live that is informed by the previous three steps. This is the pragmatic task.[27]

All this is very helpful, but what do you do when you are dealing with a unique commandment? Let me suggest that in that case

---

[25]Ibid., 269.
[26]Ibid., 270 (original emphases).
[27]Richard B. Hays, *The Moral Vision of the New Testament: A Contemporary Introduction to New Testament Ethics* (San Francisco: HarperSanFrancisco, 1996), 3–7.

the synthetic task will be more modest and will involve in particular relating that unique text to its literary unit in its book. What must be avoided, therefore, is any facile move from the command of Ephesians 5:18 to the references to the filling by the Spirit in Acts, as though to obey the command is to have the power to act like various characters in the Acts narrative (e.g., Stephen in Acts 6–7).[28]

The Pauline Command Revisited

The only place in Scripture that commands that believers be filled with or by the Spirit is in Ephesians 5:18–21, as we have seen. But no steps are enumerated, no conditions laid down as to how to obey this command. Hence the vagueness of John Stott's discussion on this matter and the filling-in-the-gaps approach of that little booklet on the Spirit-filled life that I mentioned. Consequently the proposals on how to obey differ. Here are some examples. Robert G. Gromacki argues for three conditions that need to be met, based on other Pauline texts: positively, "walk in the Spirit," and negatively, "don't grieve the Spirit" and "don't quench the Spirit."[29] If we live that way we will be filled with the Spirit. A. W. Tozer suggests four conditions that need to be met, based on a variety of New Testament texts, some Pauline and some not: "present your vessel [body]," "you must ask," "you must be willingly obedient," and "you must have faith in God."[30] According to Tozer: "This desire to be filled must become all-absorbing in your life."[31] K. Neil Foster extends the list of conditions to six: "be saved," "have a right motive," "have a deep desire to be filled," "be obedient," "put the flesh to death," and "believe God."[32]

Sometimes analogies are used to illuminate obedience to the command. One runs like this. Your life is like a house with many rooms. At conversion the Spirit comes in to take up residence. But

---

[28]For such a problematical move, see John Wimber, *Power Evangelism: Signs and Wonders Today* (London: Hodder and Stoughton, 1985), 140–41.
[29]Robert G. Gromacki, "Holy Spirit," in *Understanding Christian Theology*, ed. Charles R. Swindoll and Roy B. Zuck (Nashville, TN: Thomas Nelson, 2003), 503–4.
[30]A. W. Tozer, *The Counselor: Straight Talk about the Holy Spirit from a 20th Century Prophet* (Camp Hill, PA: Christian Publications, 1993), 80–84.
[31]Ibid., 76.
[32]K. Neill Foster, *Six Conditions for the Filling of the Holy Spirit* (Camp Hill, PA: Christian Publications, 1999), 3–13.

the question is whether the Spirit has free access to every room in the house. The living room, yes. However, what about the basement? To be filled with the Spirit the door must be opened to every room in the house. This is done through self-surrender expressed usually in some prayer to God or the Spirit. Another analogy compares obedience to the Ephesians' command to developing our lung capacity. A. M. Stibbs and J. I. Packer write:

> Now imagine a doctor telling a patient that he is not using his lungs properly, and that he needs to learn to breathe more deeply. If the patient were like some seekers after the fullness of the Spirit, his immediate reaction would be to ask the doctor to produce his lung pump, and properly fill his lungs with air for him then and there! But the doctor's prescription would be daily breathing exercises, by which he would himself learn to take in more air, and thus gradually to increase his capacity for intake. . . . Something similar applies to the Christian's experience of the fullness of the Holy Spirit. The extent to which the Spirit actually penetrates and possesses every moment of our time, every corner of our lives, and every sphere of our thought and activity, is always capable of enlargement.[33]

According to these writers, the condition to meet in order to obey the command is that of "constantly exposing ourselves to His active ministry towards us."[34] The question is whether such analogies are apt.

The textual fact, however, is that if the passage is about sanctification, no conditions and no steps are laid down in the Ephesians' text. But as Michael Griffiths points out: "How gratuitous it is, therefore, to take these verses and apply them to a crisis 'sanctification' experience. Paul describes what the Lord will do for a group of believers as they meet together."[35] And Boyd Hunt wisely comments: "No set of pre-determined conditions to the Spirit-filled life, however arduous and demanding, guarantee the fullness of the Holy Spirit. Christianity, unlike Gnosticism, teaches no secrets for

---

[33]A. M. Stibbs and J. I. Packer, *The Spirit within You: The Church's Neglected Possession* (London: Hodder and Stoughton, 1967), 60.
[34]Ibid.
[35]Michael Griffiths, *Three Men Filled with the Spirit* (London: Overseas Missionary Fellowship, 1970), 56. Griffiths's view stands in stark contrast to that of D. Martyn Lloyd-Jones, *Joy Unspeakable: The Baptism with the Holy Spirit* (Eastbourne: Kingsway Publications, 1985), 67, who ties Eph. 5:18 to the doctrine of sanctification.

persons to master in order to lead infallibly to lives of unbroken, unclouded fellowship with God."[36]

What then are we to make of this absence of conditions in the Ephesians' text?

We are asking the wrong question. The letter to the Ephesians is about the corporate life of God's people as the church, the body and, importantly for our purposes, the temple. In this great company both Jews and Gentiles have their place as the new temple of the holy God indwelt by the Spirit of God and presently under construction (Eph. 2:11–22). The unity established by Christ's death needs maintenance, though. Indeed, the Ephesians ought to be "eager to maintain the unity of the Spirit in the bond of peace" (Eph. 4:3). When they gather they are not to do so like the Gentiles do (Eph. 5:6–11). Their meetings are not to be debauched as though all were filled with wine (Eph. 5:18). Instead the Spirit is to fill them (the temple) with other-person-centered practices. With regard to these practices, they are to address one another in psalms, hymns, and spiritual songs and submit to one another out of reverence for Christ.[37] As regards the Lord Jesus himself, they are to sing and make melody in their collective heart to him, and as for the Father, they are to give thanks to him for everything. A congregation where such practices are to be found and which is motivated by other-person-centered regard, whether vertically in a Godward direction, or horizontally in a fellow believer's direction, is a Spirit-filled reality, a true temple of God. Ephesians may provide better criteria for assessing a church's health than the size of the parking lot. Imagine a gathering where the atmosphere is other-person-centered rather than consumerist, where there is real thankfulness, grateful people who truly reverence Christ and recognize one another (submit). Is such a gathering not the living temple of God?

These practices are both vertical and horizontal in direction. Making melody to the Lord is clearly vertical and submitting to

---

[36]Boyd Hunt, *Redeemed! Eschatological Redemption and the Kingdom of God* (Nashville, TN: Broadman and Holman, 1993), 62. Hunt's foil is R. A. Torrey, who delineated seven steps to the baptism of the Spirit.

[37]It is worth noting that it is difficult to distinguish between psalms, hymns, and spiritual songs. See the discussion in Gordon D. Fee, *Listening to the Spirit in the Text* (Grand Rapids, MI: Eerdmans, 2000), 102–3.

one another is obviously horizontal. We cannot simply verticalize the gathering. I have attended gatherings in certain churches where we were told that we had gathered to see Jesus only. Behind this rubric seems to be the idea that when we gather it is a rerun of the Mount of Transfiguration, where in the end the disciples only saw Jesus standing before them. I have also attended churches where the gathering was for Christian fellowship. The rationale presented was that traditional practices associated with corporate worship such as Bible reading and prayer can be done at home as an individual. However, Christian fellowship requires one another. If the more recent view of Ephesians 5:18–21 has merit, then the great apostle would have none of this. Our gathering is about God, and it is about one another.

A further question has to do with the Holy Spirit and the matter of control. The way forward here too is to take a conjunctive rather than a disjunctive approach. A congregation that is speaking to one another in the body and makes melody in its heart to the Lord and is thankful to God and submissive to one another in recognizing the roles and values of the other is under the direction of the Spirit.[38] For example, a congregation that does not recognize the place and value of children in its life and meetings is hardly under the Spirit's sway. After all, Paul sees fit to address them in their own right as bona fide participants in congregational life (Eph. 6:1–3).

A Suggestion

The command to be filled by the Spirit is passive. No specific action is called upon on our parts. Can anything more then be said? Let me venture a suggestion. I suspect that to pursue the Spirit's fullness as Stott and others recommend is misguided. Let me put it this way. If we speak to one another, make melody in our heart to the Lord,

---

[38]I take "to submit" (*hypotassein*) to mean in this context to recognize or to appreciate the role of the other in service (cf. Eph. 5:18–31; 1 Cor. 16:15–18). I note that Paul does not use submission language with regard to children and slaves (Eph. 6:1–9). Instead he uses the language of obedience (*hypakouein*). Contra Peter T. O'Brien, *The Letter to the Ephesians: The Pillar New Testament Commentary* (Leicester: Apollos, 1999), 403: "The idea of 'submission' is unpacked in v. 22 without the verb being repeated. It is as though the apostle is saying: 'submit to one another, and what I mean is, wives submit to your husbands, children to your parents, and slaves to your masters.'"

be thankful, and submit to one another out of reverence for Christ when we meet, then the Spirit indeed will control us. However, to pursue the Spirit's control is to miss it. In moral philosophy there is a fallacy called the hedonistic fallacy. Pursue pleasure, and you will not get it. Pleasure is a byproduct of other pursuits. Pursue the Spirit, and you will not be obeying the Pauline command.[39] However, fill up our gathering with these practices, and then the Spirit will be filling the temple of God. Both attitude (thankfulness and reverence or respect) and activity (speaking, singing, making melody, and so forth) are involved. Now, there is nothing mechanical about any of this. To speak to one another and to submit to one another is to be other-person-centered, not self-preoccupied. Christian *ekklēsia* is about us and the Lord. It is not about me and my consumer needs. Making melody in the heart means that this kind of congregational life is no mere form. That "heart" (*kardia*) is singular suggests that unity is a value that evangelicals need to prize.

In New Testament terms, of course, unity is not about a bland homogenizing uniformity, rather in Pauline terms it is about "the right hand of fellowship" extended and embraced (e.g., as Paul and Barnabas experienced in Jerusalem, cf. Gal. 2:9). Even so, the Pauline churches were no replicas of the one in Jerusalem.

CONCLUSION

The command to be filled by the Spirit is addressed to the congregation, not to the individual as such. It is a mistake to take this command and read the book of Acts in the light of it and maintain that if we obey the command then we will have the sort of experiences that the characters in Acts had: power, joy, and so forth. It compounds the mistake to specify conditions that must be met in order to be filled with the Spirit in obedience to Ephesians 5:18. God offers to us no twelve-step program for the individual. Rather Ephesians 5:18–21 challenges us to rethink the quality of our congregational life. Ecclesiology rather than individual sanctification is on view.

---

[39]It is interesting to observe that when the early church prayed for boldness, they were filled with the Spirit *and* became bold. They did not pray to be filled with the Spirit and have boldness as a result (Acts 4:23–31). I owe this insight to Dr. David Peterson.

Congregational life is about God and one another. For a congregation to be filled by the Spirit involves both attitudes (gratitude and reverence) and activity (speech, song, and submission). The Christian gathering is neither a concert for Christotainment, nor is it a contemporary version of the lecture hall of Tyrannus where we meet together to hear a Bible lecture—albeit without term papers. Instead it is the temple of the living God. Christ died for nothing less.

CONCLUSION

IN OUR STUDY OF THE Holy Spirit we have moved from the Gospels (blasphemy against the Spirit) to Acts (resisting the Spirit) to the Epistles (quenching, grieving, filling by the Spirit). We have traveled largely down some of the lesser-known pathways in the doctrine of the Spirit, especially in relation to certain sins against the Spirit (e.g., grieving, resisting, and quenching). Moreover, we have addressed a question not posed in Scripture at all, but raised by the prayer practice of some Christians: ought we to pray to the Holy Spirit?

The answers to our various questions may be briefly rehearsed.

How may we blaspheme against the Holy Spirit? To ascribe Jesus' healing power to Satan is to slander the Holy Spirit and is symptomatic of an attitude to God which, if it becomes fixed, leads only into never-ending darkness. The possibility of committing such a sin was not limited to the times in which Jesus walked the earth. The blasphemy against the Spirit is committed today. It is the sin of the outsider who refuses to come inside the Father's house, to which Jesus is the way (cf. John 14:6). This is a sin against the Holy Spirit because it rejects the Spirit's testimony to Jesus. Our valuation of Christ matters and it matters eternally.

How may we resist the Holy Spirit? Only in one place in the New Testament is resisting the Holy Spirit explicitly mentioned (Acts 7:51). Resisting the Spirit is how Stephen summed up Israel's consistent rejection of the Word of God in promise, law, prophecy, Jesus, and his own testimony. From the Acts narrative it is clear that Stephen's own reading of his Old Testament Scriptures in the light of Christ and his application to the attitudes and actions of his hearers was an expression of a wisdom supplied by the Holy Spirit. Resisting Stephen's words was therefore resisting the Spirit who was their source. We resist the Holy Spirit today by resisting the Word of God, which the Spirit has inspired, its faithful interpretation and application. Resistance to revelation matters.

Ought we to pray to the Holy Spirit? Christians may pray to the Spirit. Our God is the Holy Trinity. However, given that there are no biblical precedents or explicit biblical warrants, there is no obligation that the Christian pray to the Spirit. Permission, yes! Obligation, no! If a Christian never prayed to the Spirit in this life, that would not constitute a slighting or a grieving of the Spirit. But never to pray to God the Father is highly problematic. As Henri Nouwen suggests: "The whole purpose of Jesus' ministry is to bring us to the house of the Father," and, "He came to lift us up into loving community with the Father."[1] Christ is the mediator, and the Spirit is the enabler of access to the Father. The direction of our regular prayers matters.

How may we quench the Holy Spirit? The answer to that question concerns our congregational life in the first instance. When we meet we should be open to God using Christian speech to expose the moral state of our hearts. To quench the Spirit today is to ignore the preached or read Word of God that stirs our consciences, or to oppose ministries that reveal that our lives are out of moral sync with the revealed will of God. Yet we must not be naïve. Gullibility is not a Christian virtue. Not every appeal to the Holy Spirit is to be believed. Discernment matters.

How may we grieve the Holy Spirit? Grieving the Spirit can be a sad reality of both Christian corporate and individual life. The Holy Spirit is not an impersonal force or influence. The Holy Spirit is a person, the third person of the triune Godhead. Persons may be grieved. We grieve the Spirit when there is moral disparity between our espoused theology (what we say as God's people) and our operational theology (what we do). As with quenching the Spirit, the command not to grieve the Spirit is addressed to a congregation in the first instance and not to an individual. How we treat one another in the body of Christ is of great importance to God's Spirit. Interpersonal morality matters.

---

[1]Henri J. M. Nouwen, *Making All Things New: An Invitation to the Spiritual Life* (New York: HarperSanFrancisco, 1981), 50–51.

How may we be filled by the Holy Spirit? The command to be filled by the Spirit is addressed to the congregation, not to the individual as such. Accordingly, Ephesians 5:18–21 challenges us to rethink the quality of our congregational life. Ecclesiology, rather than individual sanctification or power for Christian service, is on view. Congregational life is about God and one another. It has both vertical and horizontal dimensions. For a congregation to be filled by the Spirit involves both attitudes (gratitude and reverence) and activity (speech, song, and submission). The Christian gathering is not a concert event, nor is it reducible to a classroom. Rather it is the temple of the living God. Ecclesiology matters.

GLOSSARY

Accommodatio: Lat., "accommodation," the idea that God in communicating his will and ways to humanity stoops like a great rhetorician to our level in order to connect.

Ad extra: Lat., "to the outside," a phrase used to speak of the Trinity's works of creation, revelation, and redemption.

Ad intra: Lat., "to the inside," a phrase used to speak of the Trinity's works and relations within the Godhead without any reference to created reality (e.g., the Father's love for the Son within the triune Godhead).

Biblical theology: in evangelical parlance the expression can mean either doctrine as proved by scriptural texts, or a way of using the Bible that observes the Scripture's own canonical unfolding of its story and thus places texts when used for doctrinal purposes in their contexts in their rhetorical settings in their book in the canon in the light of the flow of redemptive history. Not to be confused with the mid-twentieth century's "Biblical Theology Movement" involving liberal mainline scholars, which had largely dissipated by the end of the 1960s.

Christology: the doctrine of Christ's person and work.

Consequentialist ethics: the view that the moral value of an action depends upon its outcome.

Docetism: a Christological heresy that denies the reality of the incarnation by arguing that Christ is a spirit who only appeared or seemed (Greek, *dokein*, "to seem") to be human flesh. The Gnostic teacher Basileides is a second-century example of a docetist.

Economic Trinity: a theological expression used to speak of the various roles of the members of the Trinity in the administration (economy) of the plan of salvation. Modalistic monarchians affirm an economic Trinity of sorts as a revealed phenomenon but deny the essential Trinity.

Economy: the administration of the plan of salvation.

Eschatology: Greek, *eschaton*, "last." Traditionally narrowly defined as the "Four Last Things": death, resurrection, heaven, and hell. But increasingly a broader definition is in play as well as the narrow one. In broad definition, eschatology is the story of the unfolding of the divine purpose in time and space from creation through redemption to new creation.

Essential (or Immanent) Trinity: a theological expression used to speak of the Trinity's own eternal, internal life as Father, Son, and Holy Spirit.

External call: God's call to repentance and faith through the preaching of the gospel.

Internal call: the idea in Reformed thought that the Holy Spirit uses the external call to work in the hearts of the elect who hear to bring about repentance and faith in the gospel.

Pneumatological moments: arguably there are pneumatological moments, which parallel most of the Christological ones. "Moment" refers to an episode in the narrative of Christ that highlights some aspect of Christ's person or work, or in the case of the Spirit some aspect of the Spirit's person or work (e.g., the cross and Pentecost, respectively).

Pneumatology: the doctrine of the Holy Spirit's person and work.

Redemptive history: the plot line of the canonical revelation from old creation to new, from Genesis to Revelation with its accent on redemption.

Revelation: what God has made known about his reality, character, will, and ways.

Salvation history: see Redemptive history.

Special revelation: what God has made known about his reality, character, will, and ways to certain people at certain times (e.g., Ps. 19:7–14; Heb. 1:1–2).

SCRIPTURE INDEX